Green Pastures of Plenty

Beyond the Blue (And The Red)

Four Principles of Radical Centrism

By Dave Plassman

Dedication:

After a half century of intention I just recently read Profiles in Courage and was struck, not too surprisingly, by the eloquence and high-minded sincerity of the volume and those represented within. The reading filled me with nostalgia and a sense of humble gratitude that I had been alive at a time to observe and apprehend statesmanship. This modest work is dedicated to the memory of John Fitzgerald Kennedy and all those who answer the call of public service with dedication and honor. May we see the like again.--Dave Plassman, September 17, 2018.

Yet thank God, E'en still are beating hearts

in manhood burning noon,

Who would follow in their footsteps

at the Rising of the Moon!

From an Irish revolutionary ballad about the 1798 Rebellion.

"I desire you would Remember the Ladies, and be more generous and favorable to them than your ancestors. Do not put such unlimited power into the hands of the Husbands. Remember all Men would be tyrants if they could. If perticular care and attention is not paid to the Laidies we are determined to foment a Rebelion, and will not hold ourselves bound by any Laws in which we have no voice, or Representation. "

Abigail Adams in a letter to John, March-April 1776.)

Chapter 1.

The Conceptual Rift

The America of today is possibly divided more than ever before, at least since the North/South conflict of the 1860s, and the Western world seems to be following suit. France is factionalizing. Germany has prepared to evict foreign guest workers and nonnatives. Scotland is reconsidering its membership in the United Kingdom while the UK is withdrawing from the European Common Market.

Here in the US we are fissuring along not only political but religious, scientific, social, even emotional lines. It's not too surprising therefore that a common view of the future is essentially nonexistent, our individual aspirations too often, at angry cross-purposes with one another.

While some of us dream of reaching the stars, perhaps even "remaking them," others dream of pastoral simplicity devoid of the oppressive technocracy of the modern corporate state. (I dream of both.)

Interestingly enough, The American frontier birthed both the Space Program and the back to the land movement. On one hand visions of discovery and adventure caused a technically elite group to undertake the building of some of the most powerful machines known to humankind; a distillation of technological prowess and excellence. On the other, a larger group of savvy individuals and groups strove to sift from the past, the best our forebears bequeathed, commingled it with modern scholarship and American insight.

The Mother Earth News generation has largely passed as a major social movement. We no longer get up early or sit up late to watch a rocket launching on TV nor do we exchange with friends and neighbors, facts about space and space vehicles. (In the early 1960s we did.) Still the spirit of both social movements are very much alive and though sprung from a common root, they now stand at odds with one another.

Could the disparity between the engineering orange of high technology and the green of the Eco movement provide some clues to why the gap between red states and blue continues to widen and the animosity between nominal Liberals and Conservatives increases? Let's look at some history and do some comparisons, then perhaps we'll see if there might be available some middle ground upon which we all might stand--at least from time to time.

I grew up in the 1950s, 60s and early 70s and from an early age, thrilled to family stories of log cabins, overland stage coaches, horse-powered subsistence farms. Yet I wondered about what might lie beyond this land of America and all the other colorful places on the globe. I suppose I was bitten by the space bug even before Mercury but the flights of Alan Shepard, Gus Grissom, John Glenn and the rest, tended to give form to my early astronautical dreaming. I decided around age ten not to follow my parents' wishes for me to become a lawyer but rather to seek a career in the sciences. I held fast to this resolution and wishing to build rockets, decided upon a degree in Aerospace engineering. Along the way though I'd acquired a fascination with biological process, especially those which yield energy and allow manufacture of complex materials in modest factory settings. There wasn't all that much available in rocketry at the University of Washington during my tenure there but what I did undertake, taught me a good deal about energy. When I had term papers to turn in, they were as often as not about harnessing the sun through biological means.

Some time after I left University to seek a job, I fell in with a Seattle-based group known as the Micro Environment Research Group, or MERG, a collection of free-lance experimenters and tinkerers from disparate backgrounds. They were bound together by the general notion of constructing a more or less self-sufficient, ecologically benign community and support system which might serve as a model for others. The group centered mostly around the Heliark, a 200-foot barge anchored in Washington's Puget Sound. These folks were by now possibly neohippies because though the real Haight-Ashbury set were pretty much on the wane by the time I entered college, MERG members still ate millet and spirulina broth, sprouted bread and talked a lot about organics.

I at the time was about to make my first adult foray away from The Big City and saw in what I learned to call the back-to-the-land movement, an opportunity to use the fairly sophisticated technologies I'd learned about in engineering school; the heat engines, the solar cells, the biologically-based fuel generating processes, to give freedom and autonomy to the individual homeowner or family group. (The cowboy or girl with a horse, the homesteader with a cogenerative Stirling engine.) The idea appealed to both my pioneer roots and my high-tech tutelage from professors who consulted for Boeing or NASA.

The division that I was feeling within myself came to a sort of critical point when I was asked to attend a Campus debate at The University of Washington on high-tech Vs. Low-test energy. On one side were arrayed experts from Harvard, Livermore Labs and elsewhere, nuclear proponents to a man (no women on stage this evening.) On the other were what might be called Ecotopers from Ecological Utopia; who protested the use of aluminum foil on gum wrappers and seemed to think that solar batch water heaters and hand-turned grain mills were the answer to nuclear fission and the oil conglomerates. The university Daily didn't even cover the event.

It was so clear that the opposing sides were speaking not only *at* each other but *past* each other that I felt I needed to say something, so I stood and pointed out that there was a third way. Sophisticated technologies could be based upon biomass energy and other renewable resources and in any case, something like this would be needed even in a fission-powered economy unless hydrogen could totally supplant gasoline. I won't say I made any huge impression on anyone but I realized I both agreed and disagreed with both sides.

I certainly wasn't against roof-top solar panels and I wasn't against high technology. I knew that we not only shouldn't but *couldn't* return to a 19th century life-style, but suspected that nuclear energy would continue to be if not technologically, at least politically unfeasible and there is some good reason for the apprehension many folks feel about atomic power. In any case, I didn't seem to belong to any camp but my own. (I did cause one of the high-tech experts to mention that one could burn wheat for a nickel a kilowatt hour in 1978 dollars.)

Several years later I read a fairly fascinating and quite inspiring editorial in Analog magazine by G. Harry Stein, Physicist and science fiction writer. Doctor Stein pointed out that space advocates and proponents of the Environmental Movement complimented one another quite well. THE ecologists were good at pointing out the problems with existing technology, the hazards to human welfare and life generally. The astronautical folk were talented in devising creative solutions to complex and difficult problems. doctor Stein asked why didn't the two groups work together to create truly innovative yet safe energy sources and to construct model environments in which various life support strategies might be tested before being loosed upon the entire world or boosted into space.

Around the same time a friend of mine, one of the Merg people, commented that my interest in biomass energy with its cogenerative possibilities and interactive material flows was a way of looking ahead to the day when we would send spaceships to the outer planets or even the stars. And yes this was very insightful though I don't believe I'd put the matter in quite these terms even in my own mind. There was so much that could be accomplished if the high-tech advocates and the green tech activists could learn each other's language and settle on one or two common goals even if they disagreed about other things!

I think it was around this time that the present rift in America began to open even if it wasn't yet quite apparent. Of course Americans have been divided in one way or another (more often in several directions,) since before there really were Americans. The very two-party system upon which our government is based, assures competition and conflict and whether it's taxes, minimum wage, eminent domain or government subsidies we're always able to find something over which to squabble. Still we used to be able to get things done even if we didn't always especially like the person in the next voting booth or at the neighboring office desk. We were Americans and that counted for something.

Come 1980, Ronald Reagan was elected to his first term in The White House and things seemed now to be changing beyond the usual neighbor against neighbor bickering. I voted both times for Uncle Ron and I think he did a lot of good at the time; things that needed doing and he presented a stern face to a lot of people abroad who'd have gladly done America ill. He did also, introduce a significant element of religiosity into the US governmental system. There'd always been lip-service to religion in America at community, state and Federal levels and not a little heart-service as well, but I believe that it was during the first Reagan Administration that the concept of the Christian Right began to be manifest. It was kind of a confusing idea.

Growing up I sort of figured that most people believed in some kind of God even if not in a specific prophet or holy book. Through college and beyond I saw myself as pretty conservative, frequently referring to myself as a right-winger. My brand of Conservatism though was about getting governmental paws and snouts out of people's private affairs and freeing up entrepreneurs from excessive regulation and taxation so new things might be accomplished. Religion was something to celebrate at home, hopefully teaching our kids appropriate behavior toward themselves and one another. Now however it appeared that BIG GOVERNMENT was withdrawing resources and services from some truly needy people, including the mentally ill, while imposing moral standards generated by a comparative minority within a single religious group.

The change took a while to be perceivable. We'd always been a bit jingoistic about preferring Christianity over less acceptable religions (Okay, a *lot.)* but now ministers and TV evangelists appeared to be having as much influence over governmental processes as elected politicians and even movie stars! I think the twin issues of abortion reform and the Equal Rights Amendment was the tip of the iceberg so to speak and to mix a metaphor, of the rift between what would be seen as modern conservatism Vs. Modern Liberalism.

At this point, let's define some terms, or try to, for nobody will agree with me on every point. If we can't agree that every item mentioned, belongs on a given side of the political board, we can at least recognize that some things belong on *opposite* sides.

The term liberal used to refer to the state of being at liberty to pursue nonsubsistance-related goals as in liberal arts, studies and endeavors such as poetry, rhetoric, music, painting, logic; which were beautiful in and of themselves and for the practice of which most people had little or no opportunity. Since most people who could indulge in liberal arts were wealthy or had wealthy patrons, the term *liberal* came to mean generous or open-handed in giving.

By the time our country was founded, being a liberal such as Thomas Jefferson or James Madison, meant that one was assumed to have interests in new and innovative ideas such as reformed religion or the possibility that the races might be essentially equal. Workers might have rights. Education should be free for most of us. Voting needn't be restricted to land-owners. Of course liberalism as well as conservatism got tested sorely during the American breakaway from Britain and by the entire slave question. Feminism and Unionism also would challenge and seek to redefine what Liberals stood for, as well as prison reform, social welfare and the effort to improve the lot of persons with disabilities. Though modern Liberals speak rather little of Jefferson, Madison or Monroe I think they still see themselves as the vanguard of new ideas and generally the arbiters of fair treatment for all--or most.

It's difficult to achieve agreement as to what constitutes fairness or even social good. In order for there to be a Liberal Mindset therefore it's necessary to achieve sort of tacit agreement on what constitutes those things. In a sometimes tyrannical fashion therefore the majority of liberal-minded persons may attempt to define for everyone what our social, economic and political goals should be, in terms of Greater Good for the Majority of People. In my experience Liberals tend to be fond of asking questions beginning with 'don't you believe?' Or, 'Don't you support? Why aren't you in favor of...' This as if a cherished set of beliefs is so self-evident that no right-thinking person could possibly disagree with them. I've less often heard statements beginning with 'How did you arrive at...?' or 'what advantages do you see in...?' This doesn't make liberal ideas necessarily wrong but tends to give them the character of a secular religion, not a body of opinion drawn from life experience.

Conservatism has generally been seen as representing the status quo and the entrenched power existing during a given epoch in history. This is interesting because Cromwell and his revolutionary followers were likely much more conservative as defined today than were King Charles Stewart I and his opulent court, which by his own standards, was probably liberal-minded. Still, persons who perceive benefit from social or governmental change generally see themselves as more liberal whereas those who have a vested interest in what exists today, tend to identify more with conservatism. Most modern Conservatives I believe, see themselves as the guardians of public and private resource. They generally resist tax increases and government spending on programs and project whose benefit they view as trendy, or newfangled. This doesn't make conservative values invalid. Conservatives being generally harder to sell on any new social program often provide a counter-balance to sometimes excessive liberalism and vice versa.

Where the definitions I'm building run into trouble is in the purity of the specie or lack of same. A conservative, being focused on preserving the security of the established order may become quite liberal in spending for military purposes and since taxes should not increase, monies can be drawn from the welfare sector (the weakest and least able to self-protect sector of our society).

By the same token certain wealthy Liberals who've drawn their high-minded attitudes from privileged upbringing may associate mostly with other wealthy people and may therefore have little appreciation of the reality for impoverished people and the degree to which government function is kept occulted from the average voter. It's also true that a fiscal conservative may be quite tolerant in allowing for the opinions or life styles of others, leading some conservative persons to identify themselves as libertarians. Some very liberal persons may realize the flaw in Majority-based arguments and come to see that three thousand tyrants a mile away can be fully as odious as one tyrant three thousand miles away. (See Benjamin Martin as portrayed by Mel Gibson in The Patriot.) Such Liberals may identify as libertarians or perhaps as one or another type of radical.

So what can we do with this dichotomy of on one hand protecting the social welfare of everyone and on the other, guarding the fiscal and traditional integrity of our nation? Neither goal is bad. Neither is wholly good. Liberalism and conservatism are ever-changing quantities, more so for the former. The problem with inclusivity which has long been a cornerstone of liberal ideology is that it's so hard to keep up. When we think we've made allowances for every group or at least lavished sympathy in every necessary direction, new groups with new issues keep popping up.

Male abolitionists often found the demands of female suffragettes to be improper and ridiculous. Feminists often failed to recognize the needs and desires of their Lesbian sisters. Everyone seems to have problems with the demands of disabled groups, especially those of the blind or wheelchair users, not for social services or common charity but for the dignity afforded through an opportunity to work and be recognized as fully contributing citizens. Some straight people who had stretched their minds sufficiently to recognize and even appreciate the issues put forward by Gay groups, continued to have difficulty apprehending the real yet troubling needs of transgendered folks. Liberals have to keep reordering and reinterpreting what it means to be inclusive and correct or in a phrase, to be liberal.

The crux of this problem is the assumption that the group defines the set of individuals. In many ways it must. Men and women, gay and straight people, blind and non-ambulatory people, learning delayed, hearing impaired, all have similarities to other persons under the given definition, yet the requirements of the group is only an average thing or often the agenda of a vocal subset of that minority. It is also true that we humans are past masters at fictionalization. The history of the Protestant Churches illustrates this quite admirably. Once we accommodate one faction, several sub factions may well spring up to further concern the well-meaning inclusionary.

So do we ignore the needs of differently-oriented, differently abled, differently identifying groups of citizen neighbors or casual visitors? Of course not. We do however, need to recognize that the tendency to keep applying patches on a liberal conceptual pattern originally conceived for Straight, white, fully abled adult men is a great deal like trying to put aluminum siding on a brick house. It's necessary to get down to the basics of self-direction, safety, opportunity and dignity that should belong to every individual in a manner not referring to race, economic strata, education, sex/gender or other orientation. This is easy enough to say but how to implement? We need to examine our assumptions, define policies in the broadest possible terms and where possible, keep decision-makers unaware of what various memberships a job applicant, or prospective student might belong until empirical evidence has been gathered regarding that person's capabilities, accomplishments, and potentials. It would also be a grand idea to question not whether something should be allowed but on what principle should it be curtailed.

While Liberals ultimately have their roots in wealth and privilege Conservatives have theirs in the need to work; either themselves or requiring others to do so. There focus is apt to be security for the time-tested and assuring the mechanisms which drive our economy, military and social system. At one time everyone in a given region or belonging to a specific principality must be kept hard at some task or other or else sufficient harvested, crafted or milled commodities would not be forthcoming to keep the majority alive and reasonably healthy. We still think that way. What is that person doing standing around while the rest of us are putting in an eight to ten-hour day? It's people like that (fill in your own designation) who drag our country down and keep our taxes going up! This kind of thinking tends to set a lot of otherwise generous people against government relief programs and badly needed medical services as well as strategies for assisting workers at the bottom of the labor-market. "The minimum wage increase is going to drive me out of business and make everything cost too *much.*"

Though at one time it was essential to keep most everyone hard at work to keep the fief or kingdom operating to the satisfaction of the local knight, earl or king; there are more recently a couple of quite counter-intuitive factors in operation which fly in the face of the everybody must work and work hard doctrine. Firstly, with the coming of automation and now with the development of robotics fewer and fewer human work hours remain to be filled. Yes, as automation or roboticization increases there are more jobs for experts in automatic machinery or robot operation, but such expertise is mainly in the cerebral realm and we recall that it is easier to automate an accounting department than a janitorial service. The implication and I think, the evident reality is that we have entered an era in which there aren't enough eight-hour blocks of job-time with which to keep every qualified worker busy.

The other issue relating to basic conservative theory is a bit more esoteric and has more to do with economics than technology. When we look at the highly complex system of buying and selling, transporting, marketing, packaging and vending, upon which we all depend; it can be seen that the currency we use to transact our business, to buy and to sell whether it be paper plastic or specie, is not merely shorthand for the exchange of commodities and services between individuals and groups. Money, credit, accrued value is actually an integral component in the control system of our local, national and world markets. If sufficient currency is not in circulation to balance the various commodity and service exchanges in our socio-economic system then like a motor trying to operate on insufficient electricity, the economy must lug down and eventually stall. In essence, it takes a free sufficient flow of money through the market place to keep the business of industry healthy. If a critical number of participants have insufficient funds to buy the things that are being sold then the people producing those same things will realize diminished profits causing less to be produced. We recall that there are already insufficient hours of required work available to keep everyone fully employed. Under the old, traditional rules, where underemployment exists, poverty must follow no matter how many resources may actually be available. Now we are confronted with the rather non-conservative and not particularly compatible notion that it is preferable to "give away) money than to clog the industrially-sustaining currency flow.

Upton Sinclair proposed a solution to this dilemma which was eloquently explained in a little-known book by the science fiction writer, Robert A. Heinlein, an early adherent of Sinclair. In We the living, Heinlein's first novel, unpublished until after his death, Heinlein says in essence, If there's not enough money in circulation, we must give people membership checks, government handouts to balance currency with goods and services. This will keep the fiscal machinery running smoothly and harms no one.

For those who feel it to be immoral to give or accept anything for free, there are a couple of other options. Nowadays everybody needs something beyond secondary school in order to be successful throughout a career. We could pay people to go to school or undertake technical training. That doesn't mean everybody needs to run machines. Nurses get technical training. So do counselors. So do clerks in grocery stores. We can also make room at the bottom of the labor market for some people currently unable to find and keep jobs. We can do that by selecting some government goals aimed at the social good, (And economic prosperity,) form government operated businesses or contract with private industry. Examples might be integrated heating and electrical generating systems for private homes, solar greenhouses as residential adjuncts or the assembly of robotic systems to assist workers with sensory or physical disabilities. By training folks now in the bottom levels of the job market to step into manufacturing and organizational jobs and providing incentives for employers of lower-skilled workers to hire persons previously unemployed we could truly create new jobs without significant harm to anyone. Whenever an underutilized resource can be made to fill a need without competing with something else, wealth will result. In any case we need to stop looking at society so much as a subsistence farm and more as a life support system within which processes must balance, even if the balances struck don't always seem exactly proper, traditional or intuitive.

Having for the time being, wrung out both Liberals and Conservatives and hung each out to dry, it's appropriate to ask what all this has to do with environmentalism or astronautics? We've wandered a bit far afield but the four processes liberalism, conservatism, environmentalism and astronautics were deliberately chosen to represent some significant points. Whereas politics has been dividing us, liberal from conservative, certain technologies may work to bring us together at least locally and on some specific issues. Both astronautics especially as it relates to humans traveling in space and environmentalism appeal to the aspiration of newness and exploration characterized by the liberal viewpoint. Both technologies promise increased independence while shoring up the security of the community, which appeals to the conservative spirit.

Though certain technologies, specifically nuclear power, intercontinental missiles and much of astronautical hardware are expressions of the sophistication and might of a technocratic complex, They are also affirmations of what we can do as a technological nation and as innovative people. This kind of thing speaks well to the Federalists as well as the Jeffersonians among us.

Space technology is an integral part of the overall support system which operates to keep us alive contented and solvent. We depend upon satellites for navigation, weather forecasting, communication, entertainment; even for much of our social lives. The humanist concerns of liberal people make communication with others, the world over a thing of paramount importance, as well as the ability to minimize death and disaster from natural phenomena. Beyond satellites however is the innate drive to learn about our universe, our condition our ways of interacting with one another and by extending human experience into the extreme conditions of outer space we stand to learn much that would be difficult to apprehend in any other way. An easy example is the oft-mentioned though seldom-shared experience of looking down upon an earth with no borders.

Preparing to take a piece of our earthly environment into space forces us to understand intimately, how that environment supports us and how we interact with it. Learning to reproduce a small model of a system and make it operate smoothly is a most excellent way in which to investigate the overall system. Conservative values of national and personal security can well resonate with the desire to understand the workings of that upon which we all depend while the urge to protect the planet and life generally, is gratified by a sincere determination to understand the intricacies of ecology and the overall environment.

The back-to-the-land movement and the concern for Earth's ecosystem came largely out of the late 1960s, seeking the means to live upon the earth in a gentler fashion than the all too pervasive slash and burn methods associated with large or high-density technology. Though these movements may have begun with a desire to throw away things technological in a manner reminiscent of the Luddites, those serious practitioners sought out and refined many devices and systems which were both small, environmentally appropriate yet sophisticated. Those same practitioners often became deeply studious regarding biological processes, the processes of the earth and the care of human, animal and plant bodies. While fuel cells, solar arrays, mobile communications and computers informed the homesteader, whole food preparation, composting techniques, recycling methods and experiences in off-grid community living informs the space habitat designer (or should). In short, any trials, models or living experiences carried out in space or preparing for it, can assist people wishing to find better ways to live on the earth's surface, while whatever micro environmental knowledge we can gain either in the organic garden or the crafter's manufactury might one day, be lifted into orbit.

So does the fact that space advocates and environmentalists have commonalities necessitate any closer inter-reliance and mutual respect between traditional Liberals and traditional Conservatives? Perhaps not but yet, perhaps. Buckminster Fuller once suggested that both the American of the Soviet energy grids could be enhanced if they could be connected to one another across the Bearing Straight. With the two nations connected, helping to damp out the peaks and troughs of one another's supplies and demands and their combined generating power providing mutual security, they would become interdependent and working together would find other ways to behave as a single entity. Eventually the thought of trying to exist without one another would seem unsupportable. A pretty picture for sure and possibly workable.

Whether or not the Soviet/US conjoinment would have worked, it's fairly sure that even persons and groups with conflicting philosophies and aspirations can through the pursuit of mutually-desired projects, learn at least to seek whatever commonalty is available. If astronauts tend to be rather pro-military and ecotopists tend more to the far Left, then they can find common ground in the development of micro ecologies and global systems for third-world reduction. In this way mutual respect can be grown, a sort of connective scar tissue to bridge the wound gap between the liberal and the conservative.

Beyond the scar tissue however, how can healing continue in order to regenerate something approximating a united nation state? Deeper healing requires deeper understanding so we need to find new ways of expressing our concerns, fears, desires, aversions and to strive more assiduously to understand precisely why we disagree and if compromise is possible, then where and how. This will be the subject of the next chapter. For now however, let us at least agree and remember that we all value life, that technology both dense and defuse is necessary for the continuance of life on this globe and that neither the spacefarer nor the green activist can stand entirely on her or his own. Let us therefore supplant the red of anger and the blue of self-righteous truth with the yellow of sunlight shining there the azure sky to commingle in photosynthetic green.

Chapter 2.

Plumbing the Chasm

It is unfair to simply state that differences between religions or being religious vs. nonreligious have caused the division between ideologically opposing groups in American Politics. Religion is a factor, but one among many. Some sorts of beliefs are so basic to a given person's make-up that the reason the belief is held may be obscure though not necessarily invalid. If two groups strongly disagree on some topic or issue and a compromise must be struck it's a pretty good operating principle that to be appropriate and adequate such compromise will leave all parties feel as if something has been lost though some things have been gained. If this isn't so then it can be assumed that the accommodation is not fair or equitable to someone. Those strongly disagreeing on some important issue are unlikely to achieve entire agreement but hopefully the bitter, paralyzing impasses which have so characterized the current American political landscape, can be avoided or leastwise moderated.

Let's see how we disagree. We'll construct a list of issues that have been in the news over the last couple of decades, not exhaustive but illustrative and for each we'll designate which side of the controversy is typically seen as the Conservative viewpoint and which the liberal.

Abortion rights

This has probably been if not the number one most divisive issue in contemporary US politics, certainly among the top three. The question of whether women should receive on-demand abortions strikes at some very fundamental questions relating to definitions of life, interpretation of religion and spirituality, as well as how we view personal rights and the government's authority to infringe them. For several elections now both Democratic and Republican candidates have been getting nominated for the presidency largely due to their perceived stance on this issue. It's never fair to say that all Conservatives do such and such or all Liberals do not but, in general and the generality is a broad one, Liberals are more likely to favor abortion as a personal choice than are most Conservatives. Therefore we'll say Liberals yes, Conservatives no on abortion.

Environmentalism

It didn't really become a political issue until around 1970. Up until that time we'd been led to believe that the future would be a time of bigger, faster cars; automated homes, robotic labor and nearly free nuclear energy. What soon came to be called the Ecology Movement seen by some as synonymous with hippiedom and downright antiprogressiveness flew in the face of The American Dream. The assertion that resources were limited and we must be especially careful about what we used, how we used it and to what purposes it should be put seemed the next thing to Russian communists running our country. Interestingly enough, I as a conservative young person and a firm advocate of space development was actually in favor of the environmental movement for the most part because I saw the world as a large though not unlimited life support system. Whatever was good for spaceship operation, must in some significant sense but applicable to the earth. Still I'd have to say that though conservative ecologist is not an oxymoron; by and large Liberals will be on the yes side and Conservatives on the no.

Evolution

This continues to be an issue which affects not only our ideas of how schools should be run, but how research should be funded. This has been true at least since the time of the Scopes Trial. For a few decades it seemed that our country had reached an accommodation under which schools would teach evolution, churches could teach creationism and those of us both religious and scientific could view evolutionary processes as the hand of God in action. Since about the time of Reagan however, evolution has been under fire again with accusations that it calls into question the word of God, demeans us as humans and is merely a rival theory to Creationism as revealed in The Old Testament. Not all Conservatives are religious of course nor are all Liberals agnostic but lying so close to religious dogma, evolution tends to be a yes for the majority of Liberals and a no for a large number of Conservatives. It is certainly propaganda fodder for many candidates seeking votes from fundamentalist constituents.

Gay Marriage

It was really a non-issue for "serious politicians" until the last couple of decades because up till about the mid-70s homosexual acts were held in most places to be a priori criminal and therefore not eligible for rights protection under the law. In the 70's though, thinking about gay people changed among some influential professional groups such as the American Psychiatric

Association while at the same time, gay activists become more bold about coming forward to identify themselves as both gay and fully-participating citizens of our nation. Homosexuality was found by most medical and psychological organizations to be not in and of itself, a pathology or psychiatric disorder. It took a while to get from free choice to right to marry but now we have in several states, gay couples living legally-married lives as well as raising children with full rights of inheritance and family standing. The issue is still very controversial because again we find perceptions of religion and proper interpretation of God's word being threatened by the rights claimed by and for gay men and women. Many non-gay people have claimed their own marriages to be set at less value because they are seen now as comparable to the status granted to homosexuals, engaging in what the complainants see as sinful behavior. Again we'll have to award gay marriage a yes in the liberal camp a no in that of the Conservatives though obviously there are numerous exceptions both ways.

Healthcare reform

Medical expenses continue to rise. The number of things medicine can address increases. The emphasis of medical care is increasingly directed toward heroic measures for prolonging the lives of infirmed elderly and those suffering from morbid systemic diseases such as cancer and coronary disorders. Not only does the individual Doctor appointment keep increasing in cost but the levels of funding demanded by the medical and pharmaceutical industries continue to balloon. It's been quite a while since a single person or family wage-earner felt able to pay out of pocket for not only services rendered by the Medical provider during a specific visit but the tests ordered, and the medications and follow-up treatment prescribed.

Insurance companies found ways of offering medical coverage to potential patients on the principle that not everyone would get very sick, so medical expenses could be averaged over all the people paying medical premiums. The premiums were fed by wages either through employee benefits or individual subscription. Therefore the benefits available were a strong function of the job market. When business was down, medical benefits tended to drop. Where employment was low, fewer premium-payers existed and those with minimal wage employment or none at all, must do without or resort to public assistance. With the examples of Canada, Scandinavia and Great Britain more collectively-minded Americans have long felt that there should be some kind of system to pay medical expenses either for everyone or at least for those not able to pay for their own coverage.

Obviously to subsidize one's neighbor must ultimately cost someone else somewhere. This raises taxes, whatever the advocating politician or public health expert tells us. Things have been at crisis level with the institution of the Affordable Care Act and the subsequent pissing contest between Trump and his detractors. Universal medical care continues to be one of the bitterest conflicts items at federal and State level. Liberals who tend to think in terms of government programs to heal social ills are more likely to say yes to subsidized medical care. Conservatives characteristically suspicious of new taxes and government interference with personal choice, tend to say no.

Gun control

After the original US Constitution had been ratified, essentially establishing the United States itself, a number of additional guarantees were deemed sufficiently important to be added to the premier legal document of the nation. The revolutionary war had been fought in good part by militia especially in the early stages. Following the war, part-time citizen soldiers were still needed to protect frontier communities and to put down brushfire rebellions. We wouldn't have much of a militia without some sort of armament, so "The right of the 'people' to keep and bear arms shall not be infringed." Those who oppose private gun ownership are fond of saying that what The Founders originally intended was for the Armed Forces to be armed. Why though would we, one, raise armed forces and two, leave them unarmed? Persons opposed to any sort of gun control are fond of saying that ownership of guns in particular and possibly other sorts of weapons (the word gun is mentioned nowhere in the Bill of Rights) is the inalienable right of a free citizen. There's something to be said on both sides. At the time of the ratification of the Constitution, the time of the Highland rebellion of 1745 was little more than a generation away and the aftermath a good deal nearer. Many of our founding fathers (and mothers) came from Scotland often with a hemp necktie or worse awaiting them at home. The "Pacification" (decimation) of the Highlands made total war against highland culture including his dress, music, and any sort of weapon, down to a common dagger. Similarly in Ireland. In many other countries weapons were reserved for Nobles and their servants and forbidden to the Commons.

The US continued as a largely agrarian nation for the first century and a half of its existence. Rural people tend to hold gun ownership on a par with the possession of ploughs and axes. It was generally assumed that firearms were a general necessity for most or all people. Where gunplay got to be too much of a public nuisance, the revolver being able to deal death more handily than any previously available personal weapon; efforts were made to restrict the carrying of guns within town limits but even dwellers in large cities appreciated the need to protect themselves.

With the strengthening of police forces in most communities fewer citizens now found it necessary to protect themselves. Though the ownership of hunting weapons was generally considered to be reasonable, handguns were looked at in a more jaundiced fashion by persons who had confidence in law rather than free-enterprise self defense.

With the comparatively recent appearance of mass shootings in schools, theaters, shopping centers and other crowded areas, concern has shifted more toward the military-style assault rifle with extended magazine and retrofitable automatic features. While gun control proponents see the removal of guns from private hands to be the obvious solution to gun violence, gun ownership advocates counter that sufficient guns and magazines are in the public domain to make any effort to remove weapons from the hands and homes of private citizen will leave the law abiding at the mercy of the criminal and the terrorist. There is something to be said for both views. Canada has evidently done a pretty good job of limiting hand-guns but Canada is generally and probably for complex reasons, also a more peaceful country than the US

The restriction of private gun ownership is unlikely to solve the problems of sporadic mass shooting and localized terrorism since a great number of the guns employed in such incidents are either illegally owned or owned legally but used by someone other than the owner. As with the abortion controversy, few are willing to compromise but it's worth stating that at least two strategies offer some partial solution to these highly disturbing crimes and possibly the more generalized hand-gun style thuggery which has always been with us.

The concept of the Smart Gun which will only fire if it is very near to a bracelet, secured about the owner's wrist; is one. Used properly it could prevent Junior from stealing Dad's or Mom's handgun. The gun might even be made smarter by being fitted with a laser sight which would prevent it from firing if an object isn't sensed within 50 to 100 feet. The gun might even be deactivated by the rightful owner if it is stolen along with the accompanying bracelet.

Conservatives don't tend to like smart guns because it represents a wedge-tip in the liberal conspiracy to take all guns away from us and Liberals don't like them because after all, they're still guns. It's also true that the safer a gun becomes the less likely it is to fire, therefore there is a reliability issue. What if a battery goes dead, a laser lens gets occulted?

The other possibility is the development of a true stungun, a distance weapon which incapacitates someone in its direct line of fire, but doesn't kill. Those of us who read science fiction back in the fifties and sixties recall weapons which employed ultrasonic energy to paralyze or stun an adversary. One version was an automatic pistol firing blank cartridges forcing explosive derived gasses through a supersonic whistle! So far such a weapon has eluded inventors but I wonder about a hand-gun capable of firing miniature gas-bags; tiny versions of what we have in our cars.

Possibly delivered by air pistol, these explosive mini-balloons could deliver a knock-out punch to an attacker or other dangerous criminal. Without killing in most instances, sufficient pain or blunt force could be exerted to stop and fell.

However presented, Liberals acting for the greatest common good as they see it, tend to say yes to gun control. Conservatives, with their roots in tradition and respect for self-reliance, tend to give it a big Four-ten (*No).*

Genetic Engineering

In a sense, early growers of vegetables, grains and fruits practiced genetic engineering whenever they saved seeds from a favorite plant in hopes of growing similar ones. In the same way, causing a favorite mare and stallion or cock and hen to mate, mingling their traits can be construed as genetic engineering. The process of microscopically taking apart gene sequences and recombining them so as to produce a sort of cell which never existed before however, and getting that to replicate, can lead to totally new forms of life and unexpected changes in known forms that wouldn't be likely to arise from simple cross-breeding. What if a given strain of bean for instance much better able to flourish than any other nearby plant, escapes from the lab, and goes strangling everything else in garden and field? (Imagine the consequences!) While this scenario may not be all that likely, certain sorts of bacteria and fungi suitably modified and let go into the environment might create a menace which could overwhelm antibiotics and infect plants, animals or ourselves.

On the other hand, genetic engineering offers the prospect of much more abundant food crops useful pharmaceuticals, perhaps energy crops even wholly novel organisms useful in space exploration, containment of radioactive material or as scrubbers of chemical toxins in our environment. Like most technological advances, genetic engineering is a double-edged tool--or weapon. The specter of Michael Crichton's Andromeda Strain and the lesser-known Jon Wyndham novel Day of the Triffids is still abroad in our imaginations and nightmares. Unlike abortion and gun control, genetic engineering is a subject less easy to evaluate against the conservative-liberal dichotomy. We can infer that Conservatives, often trusting business over government programs, might well favor GE. As engineering generally tends on balance to be a fairly conservative discipline, compared say to Journalism or sociology. The degree of acceptance would likely be closely tied to how likely practical benefits are to accrue and how soon will the development pay for itself. Liberals on the other hand with their tendency toward environmental protectionism may be suspicious of such research especially if the anticipated outcomes smack significantly of military science or projects to disproportionately enrich entrenched power groups over others less entrenched or privileged.

Of course both sides would want to know about the degree of probable benefit of any given project compared to the chance of negative side-effects. I think we can assign a tentative Yes to Conservatives and a likely negative to a majority of Liberals.

Social welfare

No liberal candidate can get very high in the Federal pecking-order or those of most states without at least paying lip-service to caring for the needy. By the same token, a conservative candidate who talks too much about increasing benefits for welfare recipients will need to do some fast talking about either holding taxes constant or somehow dropping them. Though charity is as much a biblical issue as homosexuality or the sanctity of life, religious-based charity tends to associate itself with a process of giving to the petitioner what the benevolent folks feel like bestowing, often in proportion to observable expressions of gratitude from said recipient.

The concept that someone is entitled to cash, food or medical benefits just because they need them is a bit different. It is an idea which probably did more to shape liberal thinking than anything else. Conservatives though fully as capable of being generous as Liberals are more likely to perceive appropriate assistance for a neighbor or even a stranger in terms of finding that person a job. I work. Everyone else should if possible (and) why isn't the family or the church helping those who cannot? We've mentioned before that the notion that our tradition has taught us that we all must work if our country is to survive. While to a liberal, social welfare is a significant and necessary component of a responsibly-run state or nation, to a conservative social welfare represents higher taxes and failure to encourage the work ethic. I've seldom heard Liberals complain over-much about taxation and I've known many Conservatives to give quite open-handedly if they felt they had control over to what purpose and to whom they were giving. Social welfare is a probable yes for Liberals. A likely no at least beyond certain basic levels for Conservatives.

Immigration

As we hear often enough, we all came from *somewhere.* At least ethnologically so. Even First Nation folk came from somewhere else at some point. Prior to the American revolution the Colonies of the Eastern Seaboard were mostly accessible to English, Scottish and Scots Irish people with some tolerance for French, Dutch and Scandinavian people who were already here when their respective mother countries still had holdings in north America. During and after the Revolution various degrees of tolerance were found for persons from other countries, mostly European, who wished to live in a country which had declared itself to be free and not under the tyranny of any king. As the new country began to prosper, more and more people from increasingly varied parts of the world came to settle and seek their fortunes. By the time The United States had grown to a stature to rival Spain, for instance, if not yet France or England, we were monitoring and restricting the numbers of new immigrants we would accept from abroad. Quotas were imposed, evidently pegged to the size of the origin nations. Immigration quotas have caused bad feelings over the years, especially when often clandestine federal policies began to prioritize the admission of endangered former allies from various third-world conflicts.

When we speak of immigration though, we're most often these days referring to people from Mexico or some other country below the southern US border, who have arrived in the this country without benefit of quota or documentation, to work more or less unofficially in low-paying industries. Illegal immigration has been a more or less open secret often facilitated by wealthy US Citizens, those hungry for low-paid labor and there appears to be a great many people who are neither citizens nor approved for employment in the US who have nevertheless been here so long that this country has become the home of themselves as well as their children.

So what should be done? Conservative politicians tend to talk in terms of mass evictions and tightening border security. More liberal persons seem to be seeking some means of legalizing what had been illegal and allowing these illegal aliens to be approved as guest residents, eligible for naturalization and citizenship at some point. Such plans evidently place such exceptional guests ahead of many applicants who've done things the legal way. It's really unfair to talk about people being in favor of "illegal immigration" but in terms of what should be done about it, the question of whether these immigrants from Mexico or elsewhere, should be allowed to remain in the US would often draw a yes from Liberals and a frequent no from Conservatives.

Renewable energy

This is a broad topic covering just about everything except fossil fuels. Generally referring to sun, wind, tidal, biofuel and geothermal energy, it can also include space-based solar and ocean thermal generation, even nuclear, particularly hydrogen fusion. I'm not sure that anyone is truly against renewable energy per se but so far most plans for utilization of such power sources have been more expensive than the well-known oil, gas, coal and hydro sources for utility power. (Yes, hydroelectric is renewable too of course, being actually a form of solar power but we knew about it before the power dividing lines were drawn.) Alternative or renewable energy tends to arouse the apprehension of increased taxation when government gets involved and any advantage gained by solar, wind or bio, is a potential loss for the petro-chemical industry which forms a good deal of the backbone of our nation. Liberals, more likely to advocate for environmental protection and more tolerant of taxation for altruistic causes will be more likely to say yes to renewable energy while Conservatives will be more likely to say no on the grounds of practicality, cost and reliability.

Oil drilling

A companion argument to renewable energy, is the controversy over what must we do if we don't or can't sufficiently develop renewable energy sources. At this point we have few alternatives within established practice to mining more coal, drilling for more oil and gas, or damming a few more rivers but there aren't that many worth damming which have not already been. As the techno-economic system of most advanced countries have run with fair success over the last century or so through the expedient of finding and utilizing new sources of petroleum, either ours or those belonging to other nations, there is some plausibility to the argument that we should seek out new oil resources and utilize them as fully as we can. It seems that the oil must run out someday though some maverick scientists have proposed that petroleum crude might somehow be constantly regenerated within the earth by means we don't yet understand. Even if this turns out to be so, a good many of the military conflict in which our country has been involved over the last couple of generations had a great deal to do with America's increasing thirst for oil.

It's also been said that the Japanese attack on Pearl Harbor was ultimately caused because of US policy to restrict oil supplies to Japan. If America seeks to develop oil resources at home, we usually end up encroaching upon scenic natural resources such as nature preserves or upon lands held sacred to indigenous peoples. The inclusivity argument and the tendency to desire to protect the environment makes new oil drilling at home fairly unpopular among Liberals. A tendency to support the military and being more vigilant concerning national defense may make many Conservatives and especially conservative candidates relatively more pro on domestic oil drilling or the forming of alliances with oil-rich nations. For new oil drilling therefore, a qualified yes from Conservatives and a frequent no from Liberals.

Taxation

Taxation divides liberal from conservative as much as any other issue, especially at election time. It's always been that way though not always for the same reasons and not always in the same direction. Democratic Republicans, the party of Jefferson and the one which evolved into the Democratic Party, were the libertarian-leaning folks of the early nation. Federalists who resembled the contemporary GOP a good deal; were the centralized, federal control folks who wanted to build large projects, raise armies, put navies afloat. They were therefore the raise taxes folks. Nowadays Republicans tell us frequently that they'll lower taxes and sometimes they do but we generally lose services thereby. Democrats promise services and try not to talk too much about raising taxes but we're well-advised to prepare for them when such a candidate takes office. In general you can't have stuff without paying for it. Most people don't relish paying taxes. I do somewhat actually because it feels like I'm making a solid contribution to the security of my country and I'm paying something back for the large number of good things we enjoy in

America which we get whether we individually pay taxes or not. This is a great country. Increasing taxes however tend to accompany increased government. Increased government may lead to increased services but can just as easily lead to further government intrusion in our lives. Liberals therefore are more likely to say yes to some increased taxation (if reluctantly) while Conservatives will usually say no.

Hybrid automobiles

They are a partial answer to a quite venerable desire, that of a vehicle which operates reliably at highway speed but doesn't puff out clouds of hydrocarbon-laced exhaust. They aren't pure electric cars though the rechargeable variety come very close. They are something new and quite clean in vehicular autonomy. Some people choose hybrids while anticipating a 100 percent pure electric or fuel-cell driven car because they are kinder to the environment than the more conventional internal combustion system. Some prefer hybrids themselves because they're future-tending and ownership of one makes one look progressive and savvy. What about them in fact, is not to like? A fair amount evidently. Designed to be energy-efficient and carbon footprint minimal, hybrids have typically been small and not overly roomy. There's something in the American psyche which seems to cry out for large, brawny, powerful and frankly noisy vehicles which exhibit our ability to purchase gasoline and to handle heavy machinery. I'm tempted to say that this is generally a male trait but I've known a fair number of women who are attracted by the Big-vehicle SUV paradigm. The big car or truck is very traditional in any case and very American. There are of course hybrid SUVs which would seemingly defeat the original notion of owning an hybrid and I'm not sure we've got enough data yet to know if they will catch on in the rather macho-oriented truck-wielding culture. I'm not really hopeful when even emission control devices have been negatively politicized. Again it is never safe to stereotype but Liberals are more likely to say yes to hybrid autos. Conservatives at least at this point are more likely to say no.

Transgender Rights

In the footsteps of the Gay Movement has followed the quest for transgender rights. Considering how far Gay rights have come in a comparatively short time, transgender rights have taken a fairly long time to gain the level of public attention long enjoyed (or suffered) by Gay issues. It's also somewhat perplexing that transgender rights have seemed to explode on the public stage in just the last few years and are suddenly being discussed not only in the courts but also on the campaign trail. I think there are at least three reasons for this. First, though we've been hearing about transsexuality from time to time since the 1950s, the number of openly transgender people in the media and in everyday life seems to have increased (not the number of transgender folks but the percentage of that group choosing to be open about it). Second, we are today defining transgenderism and transsexuality in new ways. Transsexual (TS) used to mean someone either having accomplished a sex change or well along the way to that goal. This was the perception in the public mind even if not a psychological definition.

Nowadays, persons may call themselves transgender, transsexual, gender different, gender questioning, etc, without any serious intent to ingest hormones or seek surgery. It's harder to know what someone means when she/he say "I am transsexual." Thirdly, young people are coming out in quite public ways and parents are even increasingly; allowing sexual reassignment preparation and surgery to go ahead before the time of majority; sometimes even in the mid-teens. This is presenting society with some perplexing issues hardly dreamed of in previous generations, because we now have a significant number of young people passing through the gender barrier one way or another-- while attending school.

What are transgender rights? In a nutshell we can say the right to live from day to day in a manner that is congruent with one's self-perceived gender. Obviously if one's gender disagrees with ones medically-observed physical sex and the discrepancy is apparent, IE the person doesn't "pass" sufficiently well, confusion results in the minds of other people because an ability to decide whether someone is male or female is one of the first and most basic judgements we make when meeting a new person. Very seldom will someone say "I met a person but can't recall if it was a man or woman." A person might say "I wasn't sure," but this fact will be retained whereas dress, hair color, even facial configuration may well be forgotten.

Transgender people like everyone else like to go to the bathroom, change their clothes, be accommodated in hospitals, correctional institutions, schools, athletic activities in a manner comfortable, even critical for them, as members of their self-perceived gender.

While gay people most generally use the facilities reserved for their physiological sex, transgender people have created a situation in which someone with a penis may be in the powder room while someone with a vagina may well be in the Gents. This is confusing, distressing and offensive to a lot of people and not only for purely prejudicial reasons. Since transgenderism is no longer seen as based on a sex-change process, virtually anyone now could potentially declare self to be trans and infiltrate the other domain.

I think very few people in the "non-trans" camp are comfortable with this issue. Liberal persons who have supported gay rights may see trans rights as an extension of the same process. Conservative people who tend to value tradition are likely to find such a radical breech of social convention troublesome and even threatening. Liberals may say yes. Conservatives are likely to say no except in the case where the Conservative has evolved into that thing call Libertarian.

Defense spending

Hardly any mature person likes war, at least I hope that's true. Whether we must fight wars however and under which conditions or for what reasons we must fight are matters upon which we can certainly debate. Republican presidential candidates tend to campaign on platforms including increased defense spending and building the military. Democratic candidates tend to campaign with promises to withdraw us from current conflicts though this doesn't generally happen after the election. It's true though that one of the more liberal presidents of the 20th Century declared war on Germany, Japan and Italy with the backing of Congress and John F. Kennedy involved us in Vietnam at a combatant level though this wasn't officially recognized until Johnson's administration. In general it can be said that Conservatives are more likely to vote for candidates supporting increased defense spending and Liberals more likely to vote no, though in each case it has something to do with the nature of the conflict. The country was more or less united on Iraq when we believed weapons of mass destruction were being warehoused there. Support for President Bush II was more Republican-based when the mistake was revealed, yet Obama, fairly popular with his own party, kept us in that conflict during most of his tenure in the White House. We can say in general though, Conservatives often vote yes on increased defense spending and Liberals generally no.

Space development and exploration

This is a very broad topic including weather and navigation satellites with which hardly anyone quarrels anymore; as well as exploratory probes to other planets and beyond. Let's take human-crewed space flight as our present definition though because it's the most controversial aspect of space research and development. Who is most likely to vote yes on funding such projects as Apollo, the Shuttle and the anticipated Orion Project, and who will vote no?

Space flight generally is supremely technological so it will have appeal to many engineers and physical scientists. Though not essentially military it has military aspects and potentials. It is seen as innovative, a source of new knowledge and an expansion of the human experience which might be appealing to the liberal-minded outlook. Yet it is also seen as being in competition with efforts to clean up the environment and with social welfare programs. It also adds to the tax burden though only minimally in comparison to either defense spending or welfare allocations. In short there are reasons for Liberals and Conservatives both to like and dislike human space exploration as a social and political issue.

Thirty years ago I would suspect more Democrats would support a reasonable increase in spending for space while Republicans generally would not. Now I'm not so sure. In the most recent election very little was said by either of the leading candidates on our future in space which is strange indeed as national defense was an hotly-debated issue. The US Military is dependent upon a fleet of navigation, reconnaissance and tracking satellites which in turn depend upon Russian space taxis to get our astronauts into orbit for repairs! If any reason was ever necessary for a discussion of political views to be included in a book on space development and environmentalism, this is it! Liberals yes and no. Conservatives no and yes.

Chapter 3.

Establishing Some Principles

Now we've had a go at defining what liberalism and conservatism are in general and on which side of some issues each is likely to fall. We have Liberals tending toward yes on abortion rights, environmental protection, evolution, gay marriage, gun control healthcare reform, immigration, renewable energy, new taxation, hybrid autos, transgender rights, while Conservatives tend to be in favor only of genetic engineering, oil drilling and defense spending on our list. This isn't too surprising because Liberals tend to see themselves as being more about change while Conservatives tend to see themselves more or less as traditionalists.

Should Conservatives seem to be unfairly cast as nay-sayers though, we realize that if our labels were to switch, say gun control to gun rights, Conservatives would be a hearty yes, similarly with pro-life legislation, and free choice in medical service selection. To list my own opinions so I don't seem to be above it all, I am generally opposed to abortion, in favor of environmental protection, believe in evolution, support gay marriage, feel we need some kind of healthcare reform, generally oppose gun control, support responsible genetic engineering, support reasonable social welfare, oppose illegal immigration, support renewable energy, generally, am opposed to new oil drilling, may support reasonable new taxation, embrace hybrid autos, support transgender rights, generally support military spending, and enthusiastically support space development.

I am in favor of approximately as many things as the typical liberal though not necessarily the same things as I agree on a lot of issues with Conservatives. Here I must qualify at least three of my choices. I've said I oppose abortion but I also believe that if a woman is asked by society to bear a child then society takes on a responsibility for that child and for the health of the mother. For this reason and others, I strongly support a reasonable level of social welfare especially for pregnant mothers and their children. While I am opposed generally to gun control I must disagree with my hunting brethren and sisteren by saying that I don't see why anyone needs a semi automatic rifle with an extended clip for hunting. If as I suspect the demand for such weapons really is rooted more in the thought that we must someday fight our government then I think folks should be honest at least with themselves about this and not keep pretending that we need that sort of fire-power to fell a deer. If you do, you perhaps shouldn't be in the woods! I see nothing wrong with bolt or lever-action rifles which can also work for home defense but are less useful in a massacre. I'd like to see handguns not under gun-lock to be smartized (such can be retrofitted) or exchanged for nonlethal weapons.

Though I believe that the rights and needs of transgender persons must and should be protected and don't have an issue with a medically completed transsexual taking her or his place in the assigned social role and designations, I do have some concern about persons suddenly declaring themselves one gender or the other then willy-nilly, taking up the entitlements of the new gender role. I'm not saying this necessarily happens all that often but a great many people seem to think it does.

So having listed some of the ways in which we agree and disagree is there anything we can do with this beyond merely agreeing to disagree? I think there is something more, (not to say that anyone is right or wrong in any ultimate sense,) but there are some ways of evaluating on a somewhat objective level, how serious our various disagreements might be. This will allow us to at least try and minimize our points of contention.

Drawing inspiration from the laws of thermodynamics (there are actually four of them), we can construct the principles of social benefits/harm, principles under which we can scrutinize any issue.

The Four Principles

The first question we need to ask in evaluating a social issue is "Does the activity, action, practice really harm anyone? We may argue about it but we're moving away from opinion and more toward evidence. Whatever our answer or even if we can't find one; we should now move to the next question. "Would harm be caused if everyone participated in this activity?" If we get a yes on that, then we should ask the third question. "Though harm would be caused if a majority of people engaged in this behavior would harm result if nobody did it?" IE, some actions may be necessary in a minority of cases such as a policeman stopping a criminal, or a physician amputating a limb or an abortion being performed to save the life of the mother. The fourth principle is actually the first or "zeroeth."

The laws of thermodynamics essentially state: One, matter and energy cannot be created or destroyed though one can be changed to the other and we can't get something for nothing. Two, in converting one form of energy to another, heat into work for instance as in a steam engine, there will be some unavoidable degree of inefficiency in the process so you never get as much as you expect! Three, when things get very, very cold, the amount of randomness in a system stays constant because nothing much is happening so nothing changes.

After these laws were formulated someone went back and said "Oh yeah, Heat tends to flow from a hot place to a cold one!" and that was called "the zeroeth law of thermodynamics," which we should have thought of before everything else. In the same fashion therefore, having set down the three laws of social benefits/harm, we circle back and say 0. "Oh yeah, is there anything we can do about it in the first place?" Let's go through our list and see if our four laws do anything to change how we might look at these issues, all of which are crucial and have no simple answer.

Abortion

1: Does it hurt anybody?

Well certainly the fetus which is a person or not; depending on one's viewpoint and the age it has attained. There can also be dangers to the mother and possibly emotional hardship to her, the father or other persons.

2: Would it be a social evil if everyone had abortions?

Probably, especially with every pregnancy. 3:

If determined to be harmful in many or most cases would it but wrong if at least a few abortions were not performed? Yes. Some pregnancies endanger the mother, who is surely an already viable human being.

(And back to Zero,) Can anything be done about it?

Not really. At least we can't do anything about all abortions as long as they are available somewhere. All we can really do is prevent lower-income women from having abortions. This brings up an interesting point. Do we want to outlaw abortions per se, or refrain from forcing persons opposed to abortions, to pay for them? If the first, then we have a moral or even religious issue. If the latter, we have a social welfare debate. We'll have to give abortion a zero rating because we can't prevent all or perhaps even most of them and only a one rating if we could. (Please note that we arrived at a rating of one by starting with four and subtracting one each time we answered a question with "yes.")

Environmental protection

1: Does it hurt anyone?

Yes, to some degree, because jobs can be lost and possibly families impoverished through some measures taken to protect the environment.

2: Would it hurt if everyone did it?

Probably not because we'd have established a new way of living and new ways of mutual support.

3: skip this one because response to question two is no.

0, can we do anything about it?

Yes. Certainly. We have a yes on 1, a no on 2 and we can do something about it so we must assign our argument a value of 3.

Evolution

1: As a topic in school, does it harm anyone?

There seems to be perceived harm because the theory flies in the face of some religious beliefs.

2: Would it hurt if everyone believed in or at least studied evolutionary theory? This would largely eliminate the religious objection so, no.

3: skip this one.

0: Can we do anything about it? Evidently so. It keeps coming up for debate and acrimony. We must assign our argument a 3.

Gay Marriage

1: does it hurt anyone?

It does not appear to hurt the partners who are already self-acknowledged as gay. But some people feel their own marriages to be devalued by being compared with gay marriage so we must postulate a yes.

2: Would it be a bad thing if everyone married same-sex partners? I suspect so because most people don't appear to be gay or want to be. Yes.

3: if most people didn't engaged in same-sex marriage would it be an evil if there wasn't a minority who did?

Perhaps not to the society as a whole but the gay minority would feel harmed.

0: can we do anything about it? Yes we can make the marriages illegal so we must assign our argument a value of 1.

Genetic Engineering

1: I'm not aware of it currently hurting anyone though there is that potential so we'll have to say yes.

2: Would it be bad if everyone practiced genetic engineering?

Yes because it's a highly technical field like nuclear energy or medicine so expertise is necessary to minimize danger.

3: If genetic engineering was largely suppressed would it be an evil if no one continued working in that field?

Yes because it offers vast potential which needs exploration even if only to learn how to control it.

0: Can we do anything about it?

Yes. It's hard to curtail research entirely but stopping funding sources would slow it markedly. Argument Value 1.

Gun control

1: Yes it can harm law-abiding citizens who might have been able to defend themselves but were denied that opportunity.

2: Yes, if everyone practiced gun control harm could occur because of argument in 1, since murder or assault could still be committed in many other ways.

3: Yes. In every civilization some people are called upon to wield deadly force even if the majority is encouraged not to.

0: Can we do anything about it?

No, I believe not in the absolute sense because of the number of guns already in circulation, harvesting of which would radically change our concept of liberty. So our argument is at value at most, converted to Zero.

Healthcare Reform

1: It may do financial harm to some because of likely tax increase.

2: No, if everyone supported and participated, harm would be minimized.

3: Skip this one.

0: Can we do anything about it? Yes. So our rating is Three.

Hybrid Cars

1: Do they hurt anyone? Yes, they cause competition against conventional car manufacturers and the silence of their acceleration hasn't been well addressed so they pose a hazard to blind pedestrians.

2: No. If everyone drove one we could assume the industry to be retooled and minor flaws would be addressed.

3: Skip this one.

0: Can we do anything about it? Yes. Value 3.

Illegal immigration

1: Yes, jobs and social resources can be taken away from native or naturalized persons.

2: Yes, if everybody entered the country illegally resources could be quickly exhausted.

3: If illegal immigration was nonexistent, it would not be a social evil.

0: Can we do anything about it? Yes, though it's not clear that a wall will change the situation all that much. Value 2.

New Oil Drilling

1: Yes, it causes harm to property owners, workers, the environment generally, though it offers benefits as well.

2: Yes, if everybody drilled it would be an evil.

3: No, if major companies no longer drilled for oil it would mean that the need for petroleum was being met through some other means such as biological sources or oil-shale.

0: Can we do anything about it? Yes but it is difficult. Value of argument 2.

Renewable Energy

1: Yes, like hybrid cars, renewable energy poses competition to some entrenched energy sources and therefore to wage-earners and stockholders.

2: No, if everyone used renewable energy there would be little or no social evil because present energy companies would have found ways to retool or employees could have found work in the new energy sectors.

3: (skip)

0: Yes we can. Value of argument 3.

Space development and exploration

1: Yes, it can cause harm to astronauts as well as ground-crews during mishaps, may drop sky-junk on real estate or populace. It may take money away from more socially-based governmental programs.

2: Yes, it probably would be a bad idea if everyone did space research.

3: It would be an evil if nobody did because it is the sort of idea which must come initially from a maverick minority.

0: Can we do anything about it? Yes. Value 1.

Social Welfare

1: Yes it can put a strain on the budgets of tax-payers. It can also make it easier for some people not to look for jobs.

2: No, if everyone practiced welfare reform the problem would be shared and harm minimized.

3: (Skip)

0: Yes. Value 3.

Taxation

1: Yes, it can pose hardship to some persons responsible for paying high percentages relative to income.

2: No, if everybody paid (their share) things would balance.

3: (Skip.)

0: Yes. Value 3.

Transgender Rights

1: Yes, enforcement of certain rights for transgendered individuals appear to threaten some persons' feelings of safety and security and may pose some opportunity for crime.

2: No, if everyone believed in transgender rights we'd be in agreement and would have accommodated the needs of transgendered people without harming others.

3: (Skip)

0 Yes, though it's not always clear how. Value 3.

War Funding/defense Spending

1: Yes, war means killing, though over-reliance upon pacifism can also cause innocent lives to be lost.

2: Yes, it would be a bad thing if everyone made war by personal inclination.

3: Yes, it would probably be a social evil if force could never be leveled against groups causing threats to our security.

0: We can vote against defense spending but we've never learned to entirely avoid war so the value of this argument must be a 3changed to 0.

We've scored these items in the following way; starting with a value of 4, we subtract the number of the last question for each issue to which we respond yes. In this way a yes in item 1 and no in 2 gives a score of 3. Having gone through the initial three questions of each example we then multiply the result by either 0 or 1 depending on whether we can or cannot do anything about the behavior being examined. In this way an issue which is known to cause harm, having a value of either 3 or 2 (1) becomes 0 if we can't do anything about it.

Tallying these numbers we find that the issues fall out quite interestingly in four groups.

Those with zero scores are Abortion Rights, Gun Control and War.

Those with scores of 1 are Gay Marriage, Genetic Engineering, Space Research.

With scores of 2, illegal immigration and New Oil Drilling.

Those with scores of 3 are: Environmental Protection, Evolution

Education, Healthcare Reform, Hybrid Cars, Renewable Energy, Social Welfare, Taxation, Transgender Rights.

Ratings of zero indicate moot issues which we cannot control.

(There are also those so trivial that we really can't find anything negative about them. Would anyone be hurt if everyone wore blue socks on Tuesday? Probably not, a No in 1, would yield a score of four also but its lack of significance would suggest a zero score.) Questions to which we've assigned a score of 1 I.E. Gay Marriage, Genetic Engineering, or Space development are issues requiring an high degree of expertise, be it technical, legal or political. They tend to be fairly integral to our social and economic systems though not always accessible to everyone as individuals. Questions with scores of 2; Illegal Immigration, and New Oil Drilling; tend to be associated with special interest groups but in one way or another touch us all. Though foreign immigrants, and petroleum companies may not seem very similar, both have agendas which may be at odds with some items of national interest. The questions with scores of Three, which have elicited only one "yes" response from us, Environmental Protection, Evolution Education, Hybrid Cars, renewable energy Taxation and Transgender Rights touch us all and over which we can or should have some measure of control.

At this point some bright person is going to ask, "Why is gay marriage a One and Transgender rights a Three?" I know. I asked it myself! Some people claim to be injured or discomfited by gay marriage. Still, though not appropriate for everyone (that would constitute discrimination against heterosexuals), a comparative minority of our population appear to require same-sex marriage in order to live as safely and healthily as possible. For gay marriage to be comparable to heterosexual marriage it must offer the same advantages relative to taxes, child-custody, survivor benefits and next of kin access. It is therefore a priori a legal issue.

Some transgender rights may harm or threaten some people at level one but if nearly everyone practiced tolerance toward transgender people at level two, our culture would have undergone a significant transition (not necessarily in how we see ourselves but in how we treat one another). Transgender rights are essentially social in nature, being a process in which we are all involved and are not entirely addressable by legal, political or economic constraints.

Before moving on we should recall that it is possible to change each positive issue into a negative and vice versa then go through our analysis again to render "inverse scores." Let's do a couple of examples. What if we decided for instance that for some good and sufficient reason we wanted to ban hybrid cars. Would doing this hurt anyone? Probably. It wouldn't be good for the manufacturers of hybrids. Probably not so good for the environment either. Would it be harmful if everyone worked to ban hybrid cars? Yes, and for the same reason but cherish we have our good and sufficient reason. Assuming most hybrids were banned would it be an evil if some didn't still survived? No because of the good and sufficient reason. A few hybrids wouldn't help much with fuel saving and limiting air pollution. So, can we do anything about banning hybrids? Sure. This gives us a score of two which puts us into the special interest category. (Better check our good and sufficient reason!)

Now let's look at banning all space development. Would that be harmful? Yes, for a variety of reasons. Modern weather satellites and orbital communication systems would go the way of the auk. Would it be harmful if everyone worked to ban space development? Yes, for the same reason. If space development was generally banned, would it be an evil if there wasn't a minority doing space research development? No, because a small minority wouldn't make a difference regarding the evils of 1 and 2 and in the face of a general ban. Yes we could do something about banning space development. Again a score of 2. I am aware that my initial analysis of Space Development as a positive measure differs in the third question from what I've said in the present case. I think the difference is valid though, because in a situation where government or heavy industry is not funding space, there is no problem with individuals and small groups putting together the foundations of rocket or satellite development, which may well be of use in the future. If for some reason however, space research and development is made illegal for some reason, such as fear of being detected by hostile aliens for instance, we have a viable necessity for curtailing. A minority effort is unlikely to make an appreciable difference in the foreseeable future and might cause harm.

I won't go through all of the inverse analyses here but they're shown in appendix A. For now the scores are:

Abortion prohibition 0. (Remember.)

Eliminate environmental regulations 2.

Ban on teaching evolution in school 2.

Ban gay marriage 2.

Ban genetic engineering 2.

Assure gun rights 0.

Defund public healthcare 2.

Ban hybrid cars 2. Impose heavier immigration restrictions 2.

Ban new oil drilling 3.

Curtail renewable energy 2.

Ban space research 2.

Reduce social welfare 2.

Cut taxes 2.

Ban transgender behaviors in public 2.

Reduce defense spending 1.

Though this last one holds only if we assume everyone bans defense spending, otherwise we have a 2.

(Comparing with values in previous chart, note the increase in 2-value outcomes and reduction of 1s and 3s.

Before we move on let's look again at a 3-value, issue Transgender rights for instance. What if we wanted to totally deny transgender rights? This is pretty much the policy of many churches. So, would this hurt anyone? Yes, even if you don't believe such rights should exist you have to admit that arrests, jailings, other consequences would descend upon those unable to accept the proscription. Would it cause harm if everyone participated in the ban on trans rights? Yes, probably. If everyone participated then perhaps the problem would go away but "everyone" almost always means nearly everyone so yes some people would be harmed. If most people agreed to prevent rights for trans folk would it be a social evil if there didn't exist some people who believed in such rights? Not if the point is to ban them. Can we do anything about this? A pretty good job has been done until pretty recently and even now in many places so we have a score of 2.

At this point an interesting fact emerges. When we look at a set of issues in terms of things positive, not existing before but desired or actually coming into existence; we break down into the categories shown above. When we pose strictures or try to prevent change from the present or past status quo, we tend to converge more often toward the 2 category, because to prevent something, requires laws to be established, policing, accommodation for special interests the upholding of standards and administering exceptions. If we wish to eliminate as many abortions as possible for instance, knowing that some must be performed for reasons of saving life (that of the mother), then the arbiter of the decision becomes the doctor or the judge or the church, so we are in the special interest category instead of the social issue category (modified to zero of course.) This should not surprise us because as we've said at the outset of this chapter, Liberalism generally is expected to have to do with new ideas and tolerance whereas conservatism is supposed to have to do with traditional values and a resistance to irresponsible change. Are we therefore, offered any ways to bridge the chasm we still apprehend yawning between us?

Chapter 4.

Constructing a bridge

We began by observing the divisive animosity that appears to characterize contemporary politics in America. Then we proceeded first to a discussion of Environmentalism and high technology especially that relating to space development and how these apparently disparate areas of endeavor had often been at odds with one another during the third quarter of the 20th century. This led to the assertion that the character of politics seemed to have changed around 1980 with the dichotomy between liberal and conservative being drawn ever more deeply and starkly during the Reagan Years. This of course begged the question, "what are these entities called liberalism and conservatism?" Also, we had a go at defining them. In chapter 2 we developed a list of specific issues which appear to divide Americans at this time in our history. The list is by no means exhaustive or even uniquely significant, only a sampling of many arguments and controversies to be read, heard, streamed, experienced today. Finally we looked at a model for rating and characterizing social and socio-technical issues, not solving them but offering some perspective and to extract some qualitative and sometimes, quantitative insights about the questions posed by these issues.

Having now come from the environment and space technology, through the political landscape, if briefly; and picking up along the way some useful tools; let us loop back around to the pasture and to the spacecraft. We'll take a closer look at some Type 3 issues that we as individuals and voters may well be able to influence. We'll see if by bridging practical controversy we might create healing scar tissue to initially bridge the much deeper wound of political and social strife. America is a nation of workers. We work more and take less vacation time than any other modern industrialized nation. (Not me, necessarily, but most of us!) When we work together we can generally get along--at least until the quitting buzzer. What kinds of projects or undertakings can get America working together again politically and spiritually as well as economically and industrially?

In chapter 3 we observed that political issues tend to break down into four categories, those about which we can't do much or anything; those which require expert oversight and intervention, medicine, nuclear energy, restructuring marriage laws; those which tend to serve special interests of one sort or other, immigration, Mass Communication networks, Churches, Oil Drilling Companies; and lastly, that issues which touch all or most of us in one way or another, about which we should have some say and some control.

These are the issues for which we answered yes for question 1 in our little rating test but no on 2. This indicates that there may be some negative aspects of the issue at hand but the negative effect might well lessen if a significant percent of the population accepted and engaged in the measure or activity. Such activities might include a large-scale switch from fossil fuels to renewable energy, the adoption of hybrid automobile technology, environmental protection measures, teaching evolution in schools and transgender rights. (All on our list from chapter 2.) Additional issues of this sort might be: Affirmative action, Minimum wage, adoption of multiple official languages, Universal cash credit payments, Headstart programs for young children, free lunch programs, National Public Broadcasting, drug testing and driverless cars. While we note that not all of these issues are currently decided at the grass roots level, many of them such as

Affirmative Action and environmental protection certainly began there and perhaps more of these issues should be decided at the Polls rather than in the Legislature.

What we need is a very visible, very accessible organization which presents a third option on the political scene and with a platform of issues which are selected not to alienate either Liberals or Conservatives but to provide something positive for both. This doesn't mean that all of the hard issues should be avoided. Topics such as abortion, gun control, nuclear energy, Gay Marriage, transgender rights can be handled by presenting varying viewpoints and the scope of options available. We'll discuss this later. The specific platform items should be drawn from Value Three issues and should be presented in a novel and interesting fashion so something new is brought into the conversation. Let's take a closer look at why certain things offend Conservatives or Liberals, sometimes in a fairly visceral manner. Let us where possible, include in the agenda projects which have to do with the preservation of the Earth's ecology and the economics of energy as well as advanced manufacturing. Space development is itself a Type One issue so it is difficult to set overall space policy from the grass roots level but there are things that can be done from the small scale or popular perspective which can help nudge things in the right direction. The items on the platform should where possible, embrace the social and the artistic as well as the technological and the environmental.

A tall order, all in all, so we'd best get started! First though, let's name our movement. I'm proposing radical centrism not as a joke as in, I stay strictly right down the middle, but as an affirmation that by going to the roots of what we believe we might yet be able to reach across the gap between far left and far right to find common ground in the Heartland!

So let's look at some Type Three issues which are divisive, perhaps to Conservatives and Liberals, perhaps to scientists and nonscientists, in one or two cases to environmentalists and engineers. We'll start with teaching evolution in school.

When we speak of evolution what we generally mean is biological evolution; the idea that over a number of generations one type of organism, microbe, plant, or animal, can change its form. Some trait or set of traits endows some members of a group with such survival advantages that they reproduce more often than everybody else and over time, really significant morphologic changes can occur; flippers changing to legs and vice versa; hands developing from paws, posture becoming erect, brains growing larger, etc. Another view of evolution is that some sorts of plants, animals or mixed grouping thereof learn to cooperate and be more successful in food gathering, defending themselves raising progeny; so they survive while more solitary sorts may fail. To me this is two sides of the same coin but it teaches us that altruism can be a survival trait, not only the nature red with tooth and claw stuff. From what I apprehend there are two basic religious objections to biological evolution. The first is that a lot of people are offended by the idea of having a monkey for a grandfather. Evolutionary theory really doesn't say that. It implies that homo sapiens and the monkey came from a common root at some distant point in the past. Our common ancestor no longer exists. Still the theory says that we "came" from some other kind of creature not what we'd consider human; while it says in the Bible right there in plain Shakespearean English or Greek, Hebrew, Aramaic that Adam and Eve were created directly by God.

The second objection is that for evolution to work, we must assume processes requiring millions or hundreds of millions of years. Back around 1800 an Anglican Bishop named Berkeley added up the life spans of all of men reported in the Gospel according to Matthew starting with Adam, concluding with Jesus. This calculation lead Reverend Berkeley to set the time of creation at or close to 4004 BCE.

Since that time of course, carbon dating, potassium dating, studies of stellar evolution, fossil records, even the very rocks themselves have pretty much unanimously indicated a geological, biological and even human history much longer than six thousand years. Some people have stated that human beings and dinosaurs coexisted at some point because dinosaurs certainly existed and there wasn't sufficient time available prior to recorded history for there to have been a prehistoric age. We have dinosaur remains but the Bible says Humans existed from the Sixth Day of creation. There are a variety of theories about why carbon dating and other scientific methodology must be incorrect, some of them evidently having to do with the migration or movement of many buried objects so it seems things come from different eras when really they don't.

Others have stated that the physics behind the radioactive decay processes upon which dating is based, must be wrong. Some have said that as scientific methods become more presumptuous, God intentionally creates new evidence so researchers can delude themselves when they stray from belief in the Revealed Word. I kind of like that theory because to create a convincing hoax is sometimes more demanding than making the genuine article.

However we slice and dice things though, we seem to be left with some pretty irreconcilable differences. On one hand we have honest belief which draws from a very long tradition of teaching, discussion, meditation, prayer. On the other we have a shorter though equally vigorous tradition of observed evidence, theory, calculation, experimentation. While acceptance of biological evolution would to some people, challenge the authority of the church by undermining at least to some extent the perceived meaning of the Bible, it is also true that when a theory becomes sufficiently entrenched, reputations as well as careers can be made and lost should the theory be successfully challenged. The Theory of Evolution is called a theory because though it presents an enormous amount of evidence, it is not entirely proven. There are portions which can't be described as fact.

So what do we do in the classroom? What about a course in origins? Biological evolution could be discussed as well as Panspermia (the theory that hardy spores, wafted on stellar winds' survived the lightyears of space to land on our planet) or what evidence there may be for humans to be descendants of interplanetary voyagers. The Circadian rhythms of the human body if left to themselves are supposed to more closely match the day/night cycle of Mars than Earth. Relevant passages from the Old and New Testaments could also be included as well as passages from Islamic, Buddhist, Native American creation myths, etc. Perhaps these could be student presentations. The objective evidence for the validity of carbon 14 dating could be presented in plain language, along with some problems associated with it; and as well as a unit on geological evolution. There'd be an introduction to cosmic evolution, which would include a discussion of the significance of basic constants in nature such as *people* and energy used in rocketry calculations, to the existence of matter itself. Though biological evolution seems to chronologically challenge Judeo-Christian scripture, cosmic evolution may very well be the best evidence we have for the existence of a creator or at least the existence of something beyond the observable universe.

A course like this could include some physics as well as biology and chemistry but could be taught at about an 11th Grade level and would not constitute teaching religion in school or a disregard for anything not within the bounds of the standard evolutionary theory. Though course designs for public and private schools are typically done by experts, there's no reason why a measure could not be put up for the vote on city or county ballots, physicists, biologists, engineers, theologians, philosophers as well as illustrators and oh yes, educators; could cooperate in writing chapters of the text book and lab manual.

Next let's look at another aspect of education as well as entertainment, National Public Broadcasting (Formerly NPR), the idea that a radio or television station should be largely supported by listener contributions and benevolent grants. National Public Broadcasting radio services, which I'll single out for this example, seems to present a not entirely unique but fairly uncommon format which can attract lifelong listeners. It's not the only place where one can find classical music but it's one of the few broadcast sources of Celtic music, genuine French Music and many other kinds of ethnic music. Over the years NPR/PBS has been one of the few sources in the US for radio drama and radio variety shows complete with homey stories, hilarious and satirical sketches, even joke shows. Where else can you find game shows, puzzles on your Sunday news program or lectures from scientists, philosophers, artists?

So what's the issue if anything, with Public Broadcasting? Perhaps none, but while public radio boasts tremendous loyalty among listeners, a lot of other Americans view it with disdain or disgust. Why? Probably because it's perceived as being highly leftist in viewpoint and content. It's not hard to see how some people could get that impression. It generally is quite leftist in viewpoint as expressed by many of its program hosts and in presentations, as is evident from the style of questioning and the efforts frequently made to steer political interviewees toward the interviewer's agenda.

Well what's wrong with NPB being significantly to the political left, if indeed it is? Perhaps nothing, but while FOX News and conservative talk radio works diligently to polarize listeners to a highly right-wing viewpoint and attitude, NPB appears to be doing the same thing but in the opposite direction. Such unbalanced programming no matter in which direction it is heading contributes to the division between Liberals and Conservatives. Certainly not everyone who listens to NPB is politically to the far left. I do and I'm not. Though most of the programs which originally drew me to National Public Radio (KUOW Seattle) are no more; I still listen. I do however find myself being increasingly irritated and even angry at the growing trend among commentators of talking to persons, political figures, experts whomever in a characteristically lofty, superior fashion as if they (the interviewers) hold the only acceptable view on a given issue which can possibly exist. There is also the exasperating habit on a broadcasting network which is supposed to have a largely intellectual listenership of following presidential addresses with a hush-voiced pseudo-confidential explanation of what was just *said!* Damnit, I heard him or her and most generally I can process it for myself!

How could public radio become actually public and possibly increase membership and therefore funding? Twice a year or more, our public radio stations air a fund drive which is pretty much necessary for a system which relies significantly upon contributions from listeners. Pledges which are phoned or E-mailed in may be followed by a brief quiz on which program or programs does a listener/contributor like best. This could be taken a step further. Contributors could be invited by mail, phone or internet to specify which portion of the contribution made, is to be allocated to program A, B, C, etc. Many people won't bother but I think many would welcome the chance to make some practical difference in the amount of support their favorite show or broadcaster receives.

Of course this will be anathema to NPB programming directors because from what I can tell, they don't really give a damn about what their listeners want any more than any other broadcasting agency but the idea could be applied to a new broadcasting system open to everyone's opinions and allowing true economic democracy to subscribers. If the program doesn't make the cut, cut X. Try something else. The competition of the marketplace will evolve a programming schedule both deep in terms of content and broad in interest.

Before leaving this point I'll suggest that worse ways could be found to apportion Federal, State or Municipal taxes. Citizens could be taxed according to standards based upon income but would have the option of at least checking which categories each person wishes to support. It could be computerized through a system I've seen used for prioritizing matters in classes and workshops. Each person is given some number of gummed dots and the dots can be all used in one space or distributed in any other way. Of course dots could be electronic. (Might be fun.) Of course many people wouldn't register choices so the federal Government would be able to distribute a fair amount of funding as they do now but the final budget of the Defense Department, The National Highway system, Health Education and Welfare, Environmental Protection Agency would be fixed in part by this economic voting. Those who took advantage of the option could truly feel heard and empowered. As things stand today, issues of Tax regulation and setting of federal policy are handled by experts so must be held as Category One matters but it is about time that more of the federal power is handed back to the People.

Affirmative action: For the purposes of the present discussion we'll define this as nondiscrimination in job-hiring and school admissions. Additionally for anything which requires an application and selection process should carry with it some protection for anyone who is likely to be discriminated against for any reason besides simple lack of qualification. Affirmative action probably means a lot more in other contexts but employment and education are the most significant examples. When I was in college I heard a talk from a personnel specialist who said he'd asked an attorney for a union how could one practice legal hiring when there were mandates to hire racial minorities, women, persons over fifty, veterans and Viet Nam Era veterans. The attorney evidently told our lecturer, "Just do the best you can." Since that time we've seen gay and lesbian workers included in our definitions of fair hiring.

In 1992 the Americans with Disabilities Act was enacted into Federal Law and more recently protection for transgendered workers has been included in many places, especially State and Federal Agencies. I've even heard of a proposed bill to protect persons with unusual appearances from discrimination. While one would wish we wouldn't need such legislation, it's likely that we do. That's the problem really. We'd wish that employers wouldn't discriminate against anyone just because that person is different in some way but obviously it happens. We therefore keep making longer and longer the list of groups against which it is illegal to discriminate. No matter how lengthy the list however we never seem to embrace everyone who feels they are suffering discrimination.

For small companies it's really very hard to prevent every sort of unfair hiring. It's also pretty hard to prove when only a few workers might be hired in the course of several years. For larger companies and agencies however there is a strategy which would at least minimize opportunities for discrimination to take place. If applications on paper or online, did not ask for name, sex, racial origin, marital status or date of birth an initial screening could be conducted without risk of unfairness. In many cases a second interview might be interactive via internet. Since an increasing number of jobs today are computer-based an opportunity would be available for employers to give the prospective employee a practical exercise to evaluate the applicant's informational and analytical skills. In some cases the entire application process could be conducted in this way. Where in person interviews are crucial, hiring committees could be used and the committee should reflect the age, gender, racial and gender orientational profile of the local community. Sure there will be some shortfalls. There's always a chance that the committee won't grind finely enough and not every possible minority group will be specifically represented but the committee members will be persons expert in affirmative hiring.

There is one group or set of groups for which such hiring might be problematic in the eyes of the employer, several groups really; folks with physical, sensory, and to some extent mental health and learning difficulties. Many so-called disabled persons can function just fine in the work place if they have certain aids such as special monitors, speaking software, modified tools, seating accommodations and so forth. The ADA specifies that in companies over fourteen employees, such accommodations must be provided by the employer so this problem would seem to go away.

There can however be a question of how adequately a given accommodation strategy will enable the prospective employee. It's unfair for an employer to have to wait weeks, months or even years for an employee to get up to speed. For computer-based jobs the online hiring test with practical exercise would address this to a large degree and rehab counselors as well as rehab technology specialists could evaluate what kinds of software is being used in the job market and be in a position to advise the applicant and later the employer concerning which assistive aids, software or hardware would be most beneficial in a given situation. For non computer-related jobs objective tests might be used, I.E. can you cut out an octagonal piece of quarter-inch steel or can you run an eight-foot seam in heavy canvas.

As with educational policies, hiring practices are generally handled by experts or sometimes special-interest representatives; (area 1 or 2) but truly there is no uniform plan for applying affirmative hiring or college admission practices. Various entities use various means. For example some companies have used job redesign as a means of accommodation, assembling a set of duties of which the special needs employee is capable. Others may reserve certain jobs for employees who are blind, wheel-chair using, hearing impaired or with learning disabilities such as dyslexia. The strategy suggested here should be allowable under existing law and could be instituted by an individual employer or employment agency.

Environmental protection. If there's anything which touches everybody it is certainly the environment. Protecting it is a job which belongs to all of us. We may not be able to set national energy policy or factory emissions standards but we have a great deal of initiative possible in how we treat our garbage, heat our homes, use our water, recycle useful commodities and materials. When I was in high school the idea of recycling newspaper or soda cans was as apt to invite laughter as--voice-recognition software or cell phones! Energy shortage didn't really become an issue until the mid-70s and then it was as often as not more of an excuse for power companies and gas stations to raise rates than anything else. Probably California's frequent drought seasons led the way toward practical measures to conserve water.

From the standpoint of the individual or family the basic units of environmental impact and therefore possible protection are where we live, how we get around and where we work if we are self-employed. If we aren't self-employed then the environmental protection issues relative to our workplace is a type 2 issue (special interest), and may be largely beyond our control.

Environmental protection issues embrace what our cars, buses, subways, homes and possibly shops or offices use and what they put out. They also cover the intakes and outputs of the manufacturing processes necessary for making the things we use and disposing of the things we discard. We can't be individually responsible for all of those things but we can make some choices as to what kinds of things we use, how we use them and where those things typically end up. Everybody knows about recycling programs, low-flush toilets, double-pane windows and low-energy light bulbs. Those are all good options to use and accessible for most people. Progress is being made on low-polluting vehicles, heat pumps for home heating and cooling, even cogenerative heat and electrical power systems are becoming available. We can also make environmentally responsible choices in a lot of the things we eat, wear, consume, use construct and tend.

Of course we've all heard about eating the bulk of one's food from sources grown or produced fairly near to your home. It takes less energy to get the food to you and though you become more aware of the growing seasons in your area, you'll generally get the stuff fresher. Check out restaurants who buy locally. Learn to use as much of a fruit, vegetables, chicken, fish, as possible. Most of us can grow a little something without too much trouble even if it's a hot pepper plant in a flower pot on the window sill or bush beans in buckets on the porch, balcony, stair landing.

Since the hippie days of the Sixties people have talked about natural fibers being good for the environment. This is true as far as it goes. Cotton, linen, wool, and silk don't contain fossil fuels though may employ them for planting, harvesting etc. Some people include rayon on the list of ecologically viable fabrics but this turns out to be unwise. Though rayon is made from cellulose like silk or cotton, the chemicals used to replace the silk worms are highly polluting. Acetate is also made from cellulose and the process to manufacture it uses much more gentle and easily disposable chemicals. Acetate isn't very warming so is best used in underwear or coat linings and the like but might be chosen over nylon. While nylon is made from hydrocarbons it is more easily washed and dried than cotton or wool so the trade-offs aren't always obvious. Basically nylon and other synthetics tend to stay around a long time and might be recycled for pillow stuffing, rugs, even melted down into tiles. Cotton, rayon or even acetate can be composted, fed to goats, used for animal bedding; shredded and used as mulch. These fabrics break down rather easily and will put carbon dioxide back into the air if composted or eaten but CO_2 was taken out in the first place to make the stuff so the carbon foot print for the fiber itself is essentially neutral.

What about plastics? Some of them are recyclable and some

aren't for a fairly interesting reason. Some plastics such as polyvinyl chloride PVC, are thermal setting meaning that the chemicals which make them up lock together so once formed, can't be melted into another shape. They char instead and tend to give off noxious fumes. Other plastics such as ABS and polyethylene aren't thermal setting and can be re-melted a bunch of times. You can educate yourself on which plastics are which and of what the plastic items you use are made. Communicate with stores and other businesses you patronize and ask them to use recyclable plastics. See if you can order recyclables online. Be aware that preferring cellulose to plastics as in fast food containers isn't necessarily recycling anything. Most trash goes into landfills which are oxygen-starved environments and stuff can stay more or less intact for decades. With the CO_2 issues of today however, putting paper in landfills is just another way of locking up some carbon but it does cause more trees to be cut down which would have gone on absorbing carbon dioxide.

In his book, The Closing Circle, 1972, Barry Commoner made a fairly large point of using steel instead of aluminum because aluminum extraction required a good deal more energy per pound than steel refining. Aluminum however can be recycled in various ways, so can steel but not quite so easily. For one thing aluminum has a much lower melting temperature, 1,220 F. compared to 2600-2800. Steel is stronger in some ways than aluminum but in cases where there are fairly large cross-sections such as large diameter tubes or corrugated panels, you're pretty safe with aluminum. Aluminum combines less readily with oxygen and other corrosive elements so though it's comparatively easy to recycle it needs to be re-formed less often than steel.

The ways in which we use water or don't use it still needs a lot of work. The gray water we run down the sink or out of our washing machines contain both useful minerals and a lot of heat which is typically wasted. Some fascinating work has been done with gray-watering lawns and ornamental beds. Gray water has been used in greenhouses where it is run through gravel beds beneath the soil in growing benches to furnish not only water and nutrients but extra heat for the plants.

Speaking of lawns, this mowable green stuff is truly one of the broken links in our chain of life, trying to be circular. Grass is a hardy poly-culture consisting of a number of distinct plants which can stand up to being walked upon and keep growing. Grass covers much of our yards, those of us who have them. An acre of grass can produce several tons of dry biomass over the course of a growing year so if you have a quarter acre or so, you may well be mowing and throwing away a ton of potential biofuel or compost each summer. This uses a lot of water, contributes to landfills and takes up a lot of space which could be growing food or fiber.

If composted with dry autumn leaves, grass (being fairly nitrogen rich) can help you turn out high-quality plant food for your garden or for someone else's. Compost bins can be made from four fencing T-posts and half a roll of vinyl-coated fencing wire. Stack leaves and grass in alternating layers two-four inches thick and mix things up every couple of weeks. Add kitchen waste, vegetable trimmings, coffee grounds, tea bags and the like. Next year spread your compost over your garden in early spring to keep weeds down. That's about it.

A ton of dry grass contains about 4,600 kilowatt hours of energy, enough to run a two Kilowatt heater around the clock six months of the year. That's your heating bill. A small co-op could buy machinery to turn everyone's unwanted grass clippings into fuel pellets. Pellet-burning stoves are not overly expensive and are highly efficient.

A final note on energy; If you're using a source of fairly intense heat such as a pellet stove to heat your house, try to find ways to use the heat for more than one thing. Keep a kettle on your pellet-burner's firebox. Revive the tradition of simmering soup all day. Figure out ways to use the warm air from the stove to dry clothes. If you're presently using electricity for resistance heating (baseboards for instance) consider buying a kiln and firing things you can use or sell while you're heating your house. Making alcohol is also a possibility!

Before we leave this chapter let's take a final look at the rights (yes, and the responsibilities) of transgendered persons, especially as they relate to public facilities. We'll do this because problems presented herein are perplexing and illustrate a downside to the democratic process.

Where majority rules, minority loses, but in a culture as divided as ours has become, we must seek ways to accommodate everyone to some reasonable degree and not let it all be about some number of votes one way or the other or what the governor or president might think about it.

Masters such as these do impact us all in one way or another and ultimately, it is up to the general public to make minority groups feel heard and respected. Granted, not everyone has an interest in showing respect or consideration for certain groups which may be deemed by some to be perverse and even psychopathic. I won't engage in that specific argument at this particular time except to point out that transgenderism is not considered to be a disease by The American Psychiatric Association, nor a choice, but a condition which exists in some people, perhaps more numerous than one might think. It is possibly initiated by conditions in the womb, or perhaps programmed into our very genetic structure to occur every so often. It's a little bit like being bald or left-handed.

I can only suggest that we all think of how we'd feel if required to use a bathroom or shower belonging to folks with whom you don't identify. This and an appeal to mercy, because we all have to go sometimes, will not convince everyone but I hope that this argument will not seem trivial nor spurious.

In the Great Bathroom Debate I suspect the loudest noise is coming from the issue of male to female transsexuals, especially pre-op or not even considering-op; going into the restrooms intended for women. This is particularly problematic for a number of reasons. One being the fear that rapists or child-molesters will put on female attire and go into powder rooms to prey on women and girls. I suspect this is no more common than males targeting young boys in mens' rooms but I really have no data. There are some other concerns as well though. It's always unfair to generalize (Well, usually--) but I think it's largely true that restrooms for women are seen as a place not only to take care of the obvious functions but also as a bit of a refuge, a place to actually rest at a bad time of month or mood, even a place to socialize a bit. While I can understand this intellectually I for my own part like to speak or be spoken to in restrooms as little as possible. As a person who has suffered with shy bladder disorder since about age thirteen however, I can very well understand the desire for a safe place to pee. If someone comes into the Ladies' who doesn't look or act convincingly female, safety alarms go off and the safe calm is disturbed.

Okay, that's the view from the G.G. (Genetic Girl) side. From the standpoint of the transgendered person, in this case the male to female, post-surgical or no, I certainly don't feel safe in the men's room. I may be targeted in some way or accused of being a homosexual predator. Where *should* I go?! The points seem roughly equivalent except that the majority of American cultural history is behind the first and possibly a few or only one at any given time, behind the second. Even in psychology texts a standard way of defining a binomial variable, something that can have one of two values but never both, is the statement that all members of the set Human Beings are either male or female. (Not *so!!!*) Rare as they may be, there are a fair number of persons with sexual dimorphism and though they usually tend to identify as one or the other, some cases are questionable. It's also true that when a person is transitioning from one apparent physiological sex to another (the gender is already on target) s/he is required by medical doctors and therapists to live for a year in the sex of choice before undergoing surgery. At the beginning of that year that person may be less than convincing. At the end, hopefully more so.

Of course when someone wants very much to join a group in which she or he may not hold uncontested membership, the tendency will be to wish to accomplish all of the things perceived as constituting said membership. "I'm a girl. Girls congregate in the powder room, fix their hair, put on make-up, talk about boys or other girls where they can't be overheard, I should do likewise." The option of the third bathroom seems discriminatory, exclusionary and downright mean-spirited but it's better than requiring a person identifying psychologically and emotionally as a female to use the males only.

So the third restroom is an option though admittedly an incomplete one. Other strategies have included lowering toilet stall partitions so the stall is much more of a room than just a partitioned space. Enlarge the stalls and add a mirror and sink, you have a separate private space where you need not come into contact with anyone else. This is unsatisfactory to both the trans person and the non-trans majority users for somewhat different though largely similar reasons but again it's an option if a somewhat expensive one but we started out a hundred years ago with public restroom which were just privies built over holes in the ground and we now have handicapped/wheelchair accessible third restrooms.

I suspect we'll need a multi-tiered approach to come even close to satisfying everyone regarding this perplexing issue. Though it's embarrassing to contemplate, we need laws saying that female is to be defined as anyone with a vagina or someone in process of becoming female who has either a vagina or no classifiable genitalia while the opposite is true for defining a male. Persons under this definition would be covered with regard to the restrooms and locker rooms. Beyond this I suspect that to take an analogy from ADA, businesses restaurants or other places offering restroom facilities must have some number of full coverage compartments complete with toilet and sink, the number of which will be defined by the estimated traffic flow per average day. More and more of our shopping these days takes place in malls where restrooms are large and shared by many businesses so the cost would not be too onerous. This would allow either the trans person or the person disturbed by the possibility of sharing with trans neighbors; some privacy. Another option might be separate restrooms for young girls or young boys which have some degree of oversight but are not accessible to adults unless accompanied by children.

To what extent is all of this a Type Three issue? To the extent that we can treat one another fairly and as human beings. If the lady at the next sink looks not so much like a woman, she can be ignored or dealt with in some other non-hostile way. If someone is doing something inappropriate, we all have cell phones with cameras in them, perhaps more sophisticated electronic gadgetry. A big red panic button on the wall direct to security would also be a welcome addition for a variety of reasons, including the danger of falling on slippery tile!

Chapter 5.

Restoring the Epithelium

When a scab forms over a wound, healing is generally well underway and the advance of new Dermis or outer layer of skin can commence. In the last chapter we've looked at a number of issues in a manner containing some conservative thought, some liberal and hopefully some other which is not quite either or maybe a bit of both. Let us now go back to the beginning of Chapter 3 and see what kinds of projects the guardians of the environment and the pioneers of high technology might take on together to increase understanding between their respective cultures and to serve humanity here on earth and in space. The proposals made may not always be strictly within the realm of Option Three problems but we'll examine some strategies for giving the voter and the individual investigator influence and a role in realizing these undertakings.

Pocket Biospheres

Many of us followed with great interest the somewhat controversial though very ambitious Biosphere II project during the late 1980s, in which eight men and women lived in a sealed, three-acre dome habitat for two years, simulating a Martian mission. The project was the largest effort ever attempted to build and operate a self-sustaining environment. For those of us who are rocketeers, the enormity of the problem is in short, the problem. The idea of landing a structure over 400 feet in diameter on an extraterrestrial surface though not impossible, is (to be conservative) daunting.

There have been proposals for space craft weighing millions of tons, but not realistic in terms of anything currently under development. The Biospherian experience was fraught with a good many problems mostly centering around providing food and oxygen. Results indicated that either the large scale of the project did not help or the entire idea is unworkable. Since we already have one biosphere, the earth, we know the idea can work. Perhaps biospheres need to be bigger than three acres in extent? If so, we'd expect their crew-handling capacities to go up more rapidly than area increase, or it may be that the parts need to be put together differently. In any case if we're going to land something self-sustaining on Mars or even build such a thing within a reasonable time we'll need something much smaller, requiring less square-footage per occupant.

The basic bottle neck in environmental self-sustainability is the amount of growing surface available to produce food. That depends on the amount of light needed to drive the chemical reactions in the leaves, fronds, algae, any bio-solar collectors. Since sunlight on Mars, though not obscured by clouds or much atmosphere at all and therefore will be more reliable than on Earth, it will be less plentiful; half or less of that which falls on the Terrestrial surface. This implies a larger structure than Biosphere II if we want to support eight people and that begs the question, is it reasonable to use natural sunlight to grow our Martian food? Though I love solar energy, biomass production processes and most things that grow, I regretfully suspect not.

What else do we have? Of course at one time we'd have simply called for a nuclear reactor and grow-lights and gone racing off after Extraterrestrial adventures with sword and blaster. However, apart from some nuclear-electric generators for deep space probes, atomic power does not appear to have a near future in human space missions. One can concentrate light into a smaller area than it would otherwise have illuminated by using a geometry of mirrors like Girard O'Neill proposed for his huge orbital habitats, but to make that idea work on a planet's surface you pretty much need either something suspended overhead or a fairly complex system made up of a lot of steerable mirrors situated on high crater walls around you to get the concentrated light heading back down in the direction intended. Therefore, though it's sort of inefficient, I'm afraid our only solution is to first intercept sunlight with solar cells, and feed the electricity produced into overhead grow-lights in our habitat dome. If the dome is provided with sufficient thermal mass, such as piles of soil or rock within, the habitat could survive through the frigid Martian night and not require electrical storage for photosynthetic purposes.

So how much surface and how many solar cells are we wanting? There are a number of ways to approach this problem but some basic numbers are: if a person consumes 2,000 killocalories of food per day we must be able to generate that amount of food every day or more likely considerably more on fewer days of the year. Photosynthesis is in the order of one percent efficient in terms of light energy from the sun, converted into chemical energy in a plant. Of course most plants are not totally edible. Let's say the sun shines one third of the time on an average day. Since we'll be using artificial light and we'll set up in a sunny zone, we'll assume at least 300 days of usable sunlight per year. Let's say our plants will be selected to give us sixty percent of their mature mass as edible calories. The remainder we'll have to burn to replace water, carbon dioxide and trace growing minerals. So for each person we'll need at least 60 square meters of growing space or about 650 square feet, assuming a kilowatt of light energy is available for each square meter of green growing surface.

Fluorescent lights are becoming more and more efficient these days; so we'll assume a thirty percent efficiency which means that for each person we'll provide 200 kilowatts of electricity, eight hours per day or 1,600 for eight persons. Twelve thousand eight hundred kilowatt hours per day in all! What becomes real apparent in a hurry is that even though less than a third of this energy will ever reach the dome's interior, things are apt to become really warm. On mars this isn't such a big problem. On earth we'll want lots of rock or water to absorb unwanted heat so it can be gotten rid of through the night.

Okay, we're bold innovators, so how much solar array will we need? Assuming we can get an average of eight hours a day of useful sunlight and assuming a moderately good efficiency for our arrays, they can be more than fifteen percent but we'll take ten as our working assumption. We will need for the entire dome, sixteen thousand square meters or a square space about 415 feet on a side. That's four acres. The growing space in the dome alone will be one eighth of an acre, a dome 81 feet across. On mars the array would be bigger though not the dome. Growing food is a grandiose undertaking and it's sort of amazing that our own globe does it so handily.

We can minimize the size of our dome and it's energy array somewhat by selecting the most vigorously growing plants, perhaps genetically modified, to produce higher levels of fats, proteins and carbohydrates. We can use enzyme chemistry to convert non-digestible parts of plants into sugars and starches. By siting our experimental projects near the equator we can maximize our solar gain.

So why do this? If we are ever to land humans upon another planetary surface for a truly-extended stay we must confront the problem of food production in terms of energy consumption and sustainability. In paring down the size of experiments to model ecological processes on Earth we can ask more questions, get results sooner and allow the involvement of more numerous and diverse environmental researchers.

Ecologists without borders!

A few thoughts about content and location are also in order. On Mars we'll have to be pretty careful about water conservation for quite a while. Not so much with CO_2. There's not much air locally but what there is, consists mostly of carbon dioxide with a little nitrogen thrown in for flavoring. The loss of CO_2 which so plagued Biosphere II is the other side of oxygen loss in a recycling system. On Mars we could compress the external air and replenish any lost carbon dioxide which is a good thing since we won't be sitting in a dome all the time, we'll be venturing out in suits, exploring and building and we're not likely to compress our exhaled gasses for hauling home with us. (Gives a new meaning to holding your breath!) I think in pocket biospheres we need to focus on how much food can be grown even if we don't always keep closure, just so long as we're honest about what actually goes out and what actually comes in. That means that if we go outside for a while, we need to make up for any carbon dioxide that is lost (Just as long as we could do it on Mars.)

As we'll discuss further in chapter 6. regarding our spaceship ecology; plants don't produce everything that human beings need for continued good health so we need vitamin B12 even with the best vegetarian diet. B vitamins can be chemically synthesized. One of the points of conducting pocket biosphere projects will be to see if there are other underrepresented nutrients that green plants won't give us. Vitamin D is likely to be another one though on Mars the UV radiation is fairly high so may excite our own epidemic D generators to increased output. We can include chickens in our environment of course, or fish or rabbits, even goats and pigs but figuring five pounds per hen and at least a dozen hens to provide eggs for eight people, which is optimistic; we have sixty pounds of chicken, nearly half a person, with all that implies. Also if we want to eat chicken, butchering even a bird in a modern kitchen is already messy enough, made even more so in an environment where the water supply is limited and everything must be recycled. Perhaps over the next century Humankind will be bound together, planet to planet by the space-borne Shaklee dealer!

We should also recognize that our copious grow lights need not necessarily be solar-powered. Wind power is another prospect as is biomass fuel. We'll look at these possibilities in the next section.

The Multi-input Greenhouse

Greenhouses of course are well-known as places to grow food and onamentals and are also useful in doing ecological research. We are familiar with the concept of using solar greenhouses as collectors to gather sunlight and retain heat and we're used to operating more conventional greenhouses with utility grid electricity. Wind or biomass powered greenhouses are a bit more novel. On earth a solar greenhouse which is equipped to accept electric heat from windmills would survive very well through the winter in places where winds are strong and fairly sustained. Winds are quite powerful on Mars, even though the air is so much thinner than that of earth. It is likely that a greenhouse sited near the Martian equator with sufficient glazing and colocated with wind turbines could turn out food and process exhaled air throughout the year.

Here on earth some locales have abundant wind all of the time and some have sunlight most days of the year but almost everywhere there will be windless, cloud-covered days. Some third source of energy is needed to provide heat and light for the greenhouse during these periods. The source of choice would probably be biomass, something like grass which can be burned to run a Stirling engine or steam cycle or be biochemically processed to furnish a fuel which could operate fuel cells or an internal-combustion generator. A greenhouse sited on a grassy field could be made quite energy self-sufficient.

Okay, if we can assure energy for our growing beds throughout the year, what does that get us? It at least gives us a model for a food production system on Mars. In greenhouse air a great deal of vapor exists, which when condensed gives off a lot of heat so we have a fairly efficient heating system. Water given to the plants is also recycled through a vaporization condensation cycle so that life support function is also taken care off. If a greenhouse is about 650 square feet in extent, it can process sufficient Martian air to yield enough oxygen for one person. That's a structure only about 15 by 44 feet, a fairly small house.

Probably most importantly, a biomass-augmented sun/wind-powered greenhouse provides us with about the cheapest option available to do a spectrum of micro-environmental studies.

Whereas Biosphere II took a top-down approach by attempting to replicate the earth in miniature, the self-sustaining greenhouse provides a bottom-up option in which we start simple and add only what we must. The most basic food-growing system which I can think of for a greenhouse environment would be grain, legumes and greens. Buckwheat would be a good choice for a grain. It has a high yield and is a nitrogen fixer. Soya also fixes nitrogen in the soil and can be eaten green, matured and dried, ground into flour or processed into soya milk or tofu. For all the bad press tofu gets, it is probably one of the most versatile foods there is and can be made into anything from eggless scramble to ice cream. Greens such as lettuce, spinach, beets, onions all love nitrogen and provide *salad!* something that will be craved by anyone living on a diet of mainly grain and beans. Of course there are many other varieties of grain-legume combinations which can be tried.

Once the three basic crops are established in soil or hydroponic tanks we can add one factor at a time to see how many components we need to make the system work more or less indefinitely. Must we compost the parts of the plants we don't eat or can we burn them it and return the ash to the soil or water? If we're growing in soil, how necessary are earthworms? Can we reasonably hand pollinate our plants or must we introduce a hive of bees? Of course questions like these have been asked many times before but I think our databases relating to recycling greenhouses with independent power supplies are fairly short on practical content. Anyone can build a test greenhouse. It needn't support a person. A couple of chickens will do and if it stays in operation for a year or two, it in its way will furnish information as valuable as that given us by Biosphere Ii.

The promise of Algae

In the early days of astronautics there was a lot of discussion and research concerning the problem of how to feed astronauts on deep space missions. Some sixty years later we've still not sent anyone into truly Deep Space but the questions still remain and not that much changed from when originally posed. As we've seen above, raising food is an energy and space intensive proposition and the idea of trying to loft a cornfield seems pretty daunting. Algae looked like the solution to the major nutritional needs of astronauts and possibly people here on earth, because it can have a per acre yield several times that of most land crops. It turns out that for rocket-propelled missions of long duration if the rockets are powered by nuclear, solar or beamed energy, it makes more sense to take along frozen prepared meals and combust our resulting metabolic output to carbon dioxide and water to be used as reaction mass. Still at some point for space stations or certainly space colonies, we'll want near if not total recycling of waste products back into food. How reasonable then is algae as a primary food source?

Spirulina, which appears to be the drug of choice on the nutritional algae scene and has been for quite some time; has a high protein content, a spectrum of vitamins and minerals and all of it is digestible. It's also pretty low in fats and carbohydrates. You'd need to eat about a pound of the stuff to get your daily caloric needs met and it would be rather like an Atkins Diet. Algae could be modified genetically to produce more fats and carbohydrates than spirulina currently offers and this would be an excellent project for addressing both nutritional concerns here at home and in space. Also, some forms of algae contain significant amounts of oil though they may not be the most nutritional sort. Learning more about how to enhance algae's oil content would be worthwhile to the biofuel industry as well as for nutritional purposes.

Having said the foregoing I must remark that algae Spirulina or other; does seem unlikely as a total or even primary food source for long periods of time. I've eaten a few grams of it from time to time and usually with a lot of supportive material. My wife and I made green eggs and ham once--only once. The algae has a strong sort of minerally, mushroomy flavor that tends to stay with you a long while after breakfast. Spirulina can be baked into breads or dried into fruit leathers. A tasty drink can also be made with water, molasses, lemon juice, chili pepper and a little salt. A blender full of water however uses up only about half an ounce of the algae. I do think a lot more research than I've been able to find out about needs to go into how to actually *eat* larger amounts of algae and I think we'll need an additional source of carbohydrates and there is always the lack of roughage problem. It's not clear also if algae generates a full spectrum of B vitamins.

Doing algae research in isolated bioreactors in which all conditions can be controlled will but an excellent application of genetic engineering as well as closed system ecology. There will be no significant danger of a monster algal cell getting loose in the swamp or the ocean and taking over the planet! Can humans coexist in symbiosis with an algae culture? Can we reduce our waste products to a form in which the algae can ingest and utilize, in order to freshen the air and furnish nutritional biomass? Research has been done but not enough.

In the early Sixties NASA had a project underway called Oasis in which it was proposed to use solar energy to grow algae and use a fungal culture to break down and absorb nutrients from sewage, creating a sort of lichen culture with the human being included in the interaction. I'd like to see something like this revived and there's no reason it needs to be particularly expensive.

For reasons we'll soon explore, any reasonable colonization of Mars will begin on one or both of the Martian moons. While it's possible to extract oxygen from rock, hydrogen will be in short supply in these locales. From my perspective the most reasonable means of resupplying crew members on an asteroid or a Martian moon would be to use very light weight tanks of liquid hydrogen with large concentrating mirrors attached, (perhaps balloons silvered on one hemisphere and inflated with hydrogen gas to maintain their shape.)

A small solar thermal rocket would drive the craft to its destination, at which point residual hydrogen in the solar concentrators would be reacted with rock-derived oxygen (as well as the tankage itself). Specially formulated to burn completely, the plastic tanking and balloon material would provide water for the crew's needs as well as carbon dioxide which could be stored initially but in time, used to grow first an algae culture and later something perhaps like sunflowers or amaranth grown under domes or in film-covered pits in the rock of the Martian moon. Ultimately the more carbon we can store, the larger we can grow our colony and include perhaps, meat, egg and even milk-producing animals.

We see now that algae research is closely-related not only to nutrition, air purification and alternative fuels but plastics development and probably the entire process of deep space colonization. It also turns out that algae can grow using the output of coal-fired power plants as their CO2 source and the waste heat from the generating process to keep the growing culture warm. Knowing these things we can investigate which sorts of plastics, burned in pure oxygen, will yield combustion products appropriate to feed the algae culture. All these lines of research provide ample scope of inquiry for the ecologist as well as the space systems engineer.

The gravity dumbbell

Let's stay out here in orbit for a while, whether it be in a wholly free-floating satellite or one moored to a large rock furnishing us only with micro gravity. The question is, how long can we do so, and should we? When people were writing about space travel back in so decades before any of it had happened, readers were frequently regaled with accounts of the great fun one could have in free fall and some authors looked forward to a time when generations of human beings might live in weightlessness throughout their lives. Around the time of Apollo, those of us here on earth began to get a glimmering that weightlessness was perhaps not all it was cracked up to be. Calcium loss from bones we were told, would happen during prolonged exposure as well as muscle atrophy. The sense of balance was impaired. Astronaut's felt like they had a head cold all of the time. Even the sense of taste was messed up.

It looks like the free-floating ships and stations of Arthur Clarke and Robert Heinlein are not workable as long term prospects but we know very little about partial loss of gravity, gravitational forces less than that experienced on Earth. Astronauts have remained on the moon only a couple days at most and though an experiment with centrifugal gravity was conducted during Gemini when we had two capsules in earth orbit at the same time, very little has been done to investigate what the human body's reaction is to a fraction of a G. We know that it's possible to simulate whatever level of gravity we want by spinning an object about its axis or having two objects at opposite ends of a tether spinning about its common center as with the Gemini trial. The more gravity you want to produce the longer the tether you'll want and the faster the spin.

Experts seem to agree that in an environment from which people wish to observe anything external, much more than one rotation per minute is risky for most people. Also there are unsettling effects if one is being spun on too short a radius because one's feet weigh more proportionally than one's head. They are also traveling at different speeds with respect to one another which causes vestibular and sensory problems. To produce one gravity at an angular velocity of no more than one RMP therefore we need something with a diameter of rather more than a mile.

It is not known if low gravity is intrinsically deleterious to human body function. One would need to exercise of course to keep fit under reduced gravity but that's not too big a problem. It may be that the mammalian organism just needs to know which end is up for the most part and, given workouts, can survive perhaps forever under, say, the Moon's gravity. The point is pretty important because as we've often heard, some people suffering from heart disease or invaliding conditions may in the near future wish to live out their lives in a low-gravity environment.

So what sort of diameter do we need to accomplish one sixth of Earth's normal gravity at one revolution per minute? It works out to right around 900 feet. That's still a goodly distance but with modern high-tensile fibers such as Kevlar, we could tie two habitat modules together with a line massing only a few kilos. When I was a teenager drawing up my master plan for the conquest of space I envisioned as a fairly early step, a spacecraft called The Honeymoon Module. I imagined a man and woman probably, sharing two compartments at opposite ends of a connecting framework, possibly with the drive system at the center of gravity between. Passage between the modules would be through a long, flexible plastic tunnel, perhaps just a long plastic bag filled with air. SpaceX is now able to launch payloads of three tons or more into earth orbit and plans are underway to send humans. Other aerospace companies are also entering the field. Two modules, orbital capsules, each with one or two persons aboard, linked at a suitable distance and set spinning about the common center of mass via steering rockets, would be a suitable environment in which to begin our studies of low-gravity on humans. Eventually it would be good to have a permanent station, two modules weighing perhaps fifteen tons apiece and with some deck space on which to walk around and exercise; spinning dumbbell fashion in near earth orbit. The needful thing at this point is to get *something* (two somethings) up there and spinning; at least for a few days. While this project is mostly of interest to the spacefarers among us, any knowledge of what effect gravity has upon the human body can be of use to medicine as well as to ecology because it will show us more about how our earth environment supports us.

If we travel to Mars under weightless conditions, human voyagers will arrive with essentially no sense of balance and will likely be suffering all of the other medical conditions mentioned above. The only sensible thing to do would be to make the voyage under partial gravity or spend recuperation time in a Phobos or Deimos-based centrifugal station, perhaps rotating about a pylon stuck into the Martian moon's surface and kept rotating on some sort of magnetic bearing. Such a station could also be provided with a radiation storm cellar, perhaps dug with shaped charges and shielded on the mouth end with bags of rubble, to protect against solar flares.

How fast would the station need to spin? It appears we don't know before we conduct a fair number of experiments, but even one could teach us something important. What can we, as voters, do about it? Well lotteries are popular these days. I see nothing wrong with setting up a space lottery, paying prizes like the Government variety; which would allow prize money to accumulate. This would be awarded to the first group who puts two capsules in orbit which are set rotating about one another furnishing at least five feet per second squared centrifugal acceleration, and which can support at least two human test subjects for a period of 72 hours. Once the test subjects have landed, there should be no shortage of scientific interest in testing how they've fared during the experiment. Once any principle is tested, it can be repeated. I don't see how we can go to Mars without it!

Another Look at Telepresence

An idea that Robert Heinlein presented in his short novel Waldo and Arthur C. Clarke discussed in his seminal book Profiles of the Future is that of transmitting sensory data from a remote location to our own body or brain while returning instructions for motions to be effected at the distant location. If a robot equipped with humanlike hands were positioned somewhere across town or across the continent for instance, we could slip our hands into a set of sensory gloves and looking stereoscopically out of the robot's eyes, could in theory, perform any task at a distance that we could carry out with our own hands at home. It turns out that hands are really pretty complex and delicate things to try to duplicate especially for use in hostile environments. Even two sets of lobster claws though, operated by thumb and finger can accomplish a great deal. We'll need something like this if we plan a serious building project on Mars and probably even the Moon.

While someone completing a crossing from Earth to Mars or some other deep space objective may not immediately be in condition to make a landing and walk around on the planet's surface, he or she could sit in a command chair and operate a telepresence bot by remote control. Such machines under human direction should be able to accomplish anything space suited astronaut explorers can. A bit nearer to home, we'll want to do a lot of specialized operations on the moon if we ever get a lunar base established and though there is a significant time lag, (about three seconds round trip) between the Earth and Luna; slow, deliberate telepresence operations should be able to provide expert specialist services to the onsite staff of the base. doctor Jerry Pournelle proposed this back around 1981 in one of his science columns for Galaxy Magazine. Earth surface to high orbit link-ups might well be used to make repairs and undertake new construction in places where it would be too inconvenient, expensive or dangerous to send people.

The sensitivity and resolution possible to our human fingertips is well beyond the capability of similar robotic appendages but I found many years ago that I could determine a great deal of detail about an object using fingertips with only sixteen touch cells per digit. even two fingers and a thumb, the thumb needing less sensitivity; would cut the data load between human operator and extensional device to a reasonable level and our robotic hands could be quite robust, probably actuated with cables and electric servo motors though tiny pistons fueled by hydrogen peroxide might actually work better.

When we have a robot both flexible enough and sufficiently simple that it can be made to assemble a copy of itself, a sort of holy grail in robotics will have been achieved. (See next section.)

From the minimum component/maximum flexibility bot we can build in ever more complexity and sensitivity and instead of receiving feed-back from our remote devices through tiny vibrators in our gloves we may well in not too many years, be able to *feel* what the robot does through the cortex of our brains. When that happens the way will be open to not only immerse truly into a virtual reality environment but even to live what someone else of a different age, sex, ability set experiences in everyday life or achieving some triumph at the top of Mount Everest or the bottom of the sea. It may well be possible even to experience weightlessness in the comfort of your living room.

The contribution Telepresence can make here on earth is to largely eliminate much of the across town and cross-country transporting we do, sometimes for pretty trivial reasons. We're not talking about eliminating social groupings or pleasure trips, even junkets which truly call for onsite human presence but a lot of unnecessary traffic will go away, along with fuel burned and risk of collisions and traffic fatalities.

These are far from new ideas but the technological pieces of the puzzle seem now to be just about poised for being put in place and much of the work can be done in a home workshop or a small university's tech labs. We need people who understand skin and the sense of touch as well as small-scale power applications and robotic linkages. One of my professors once told me that he felt that dropping the atomic bomb, as terrible as that was, did more to get the various types of scientists talking together than anything else. He said the physicist and the biologist had to get together to understand what radiation did to living things. The chemist and the epidemiologist and the ecologist needed to get together to find out what radioactive materials did to the environment and even the industrial psychologist had to get together with the nuclear safety specialist to determine how vigilant a crew of monitoring personnel could be expected to remain, and what extent does the degree of risk on a job affect the focus an individual can maintain over an extended period? Is there such a thing as too safe?

Telepresence need involve nothing like dropping bombs, nuclear or otherwise. It need not involve anything truly terrible at all though they could. Still it's hard to find a specific area of research and development that could involve more fields of study and more varieties of scientists, engineers, social scientists and artists.

Fabber for the Home, Fabber for the Future

The other side of the minipart/versatile telepresence robot in the self-reproducing loop is machine fabbing. That means the creation of single units, of actual machines with embedded wiring, working motors and moving parts. It's possible to build up a pretty flexible robot from about a dozen parts if each of those parts have electric motors formed into them. A thesis project at Cornell university has involved fabricating little robots which could walk out of the 3-D printer on their own.

Everybody knows by now about layered manufacturing, freeform fabrication, 3-Do printing. A layer of powder or melted material is laid down to form a horizontal cross section of whatever you want to build. The powder is melted or the extruded material is allowed to set, then a new layer is applied. Fabbing enthusiasts are fond of saying their machines can make pretty much anything. That's sort of true if by "thing" you mean a single component, artifact; usually made from plastic. Anything beyond that requires either a much more expensive system or the same sort of hands-on assembly we use for any other kind of manufacturing.

The key to truly sophisticated fabbing relies on the ability to do 3-Do printing with at least four materials simultaneous, A ferromagnetic, a conductor, an insulator and a barrier material such as oil to keep mechanical components distinct from one another. If you think of building up something from very fine sand, iron and aluminum, powders along with machine oil you'd have the idea. There are a couple of ways to fab with several different species of material. One is to use a process rather like Xerography to lay down successive patterns of one sort of powder then another, flash heat the layer with microwaves then do another layer. The other, somewhat clunkier method that I know about, is to lay down a mask of paper, laser cut a shape and lift it out to form a shallow, dammed enclosure or indention into which powder can be spread, then further laser cuttings might be made, more paper pulled out of the way and a different powder applied, probably with sinterings by laser or microwave for each region on the same layer. This method would leave a lot of cellulose embedded in or surrounding what we're making. There are various ways by which this might be removed but in some cases it could act as a useful insulating material or through the use of some between-the-layers glue, could create a wood-like housing.

The environmental benefits of the fabber are numerous but two of them stand out. Since we're building up items and not cutting them from blanks of stock, metal plastic etc. we process and waste less material. Also since fabbers are electric and need not necessarily run on anybody's schedule but their own; they could take advantage of what might be called punctuated production, which means that when the sun is out the fabber will run. Fed by its internal coding, it chugs away at whatever it is set to do. When the sun goes away, the system goes into a rest mode. No storage batteries, no fuel need be burned.

For space development the fabber is needed for a number of reasons. It'll probably be useful for making the kinds of telepresence devices we've already discussed and it and the bots it can create, along with its own replacement parts, would constitute a self-assembling system; the dream of the roboticist and the technological futurist. We also need fabbers to help us make photo-voltaic cells from Lunar regolith as most major space enterprises of the next century or two will depend on the ability to construct very large arrays of solar cells on the moon, on Mars or in various orbits. We'll start here on earth building power arrays for pocket biospheres. The third application is for making spare parts for the Martian and asteroid expeditions; though as pointed out previously, spare parts may actually mean spare machines. When our fabbers can replace a hardware store instead of merely a sand-casting operation, we'll have ushered in a true revolution in technology.

Fabbers have a potential for use in the average home but I suspect not in their present form. When people talk about using a home fabber they tend to mention ordering up clean underwear, food items and other soft commodities. These things are rather beyond the capacity of the lower to medium-cost plastic filament or ink-spray-based systems currently available. I've compiled a list of the top hundred things I'd want from a fabber within a given week. The majority of the things I came up with were fiber-based such as clothing items or cleaning supplies as well as things like soap deodorant and some light utensils. I postulated that a system able to lay down cellulose and plastic powders as well as dispensing mil on water-based substances might potentially be used to create clothing, paper items cosmetics and even food items. A common-interest project for the home economist and the fabbing researcher can be the development of a set of fabrics, perhaps composed of finely-divided cellulose powder, glued together with powdered nylon which can be printed to various layers so a folded finished garment emerges from the fabbing machine.

Neogreen - artificial photosynthesis

Though in space the energies of choice will likely be electric and very high temperature thermal; here on earth we need something more storable and portable. A station in orbit or on the moon can predict with utter certainty when sunlight will be available and in what amount. Not so at the bottom of Earth's atmosphere with its cloud covering, and other randomizing effects. As in space electricity is probably the most convenient energy form here on earth but electrical utilization tends to tie us to centralized generation plants which can be polluting and are quite consumptive of natural resources whether petroleum, coal, natural gas or falling water. Solar and wind energy are appropriate energy sources for households or farmsteads but when it's not available we're dependent upon stored energy in thermal form, battery charge or some other storage medium, generally heavy, bulky and not particularly portable. Green plants of course store sun energy and can be processed to yield a variety of fuels but as we've seen, their sunlight to biomass conversion efficiency is quite low. While photo-voltaic cells can be used to split water, giving us storable hydrogen as well as pure oxygen to bubble through our swimming pool or burn things more efficiently; the apparatus to do so is pretty expensive and risking hydrogen gas leaks isn't a very pleasant prospect. A possible alternative is glimpsed in artificial photosynthesis.

This is basically a set of reactions employing semiconductors, catalysts and other molecular wizardry to mimic what photosynthesis does or to do something like it. Photosynthesis breaks down water and carbon dioxide to form glucose molecules and free oxygen. The glucose goes on to build up an host of more complex molecules and structures. Artificial photosynthesis may employ compounds such as titanium dioxide $TiO2$. iron compounds, or things more exotic to split water into hydrogen and oxygen, carbon dioxide into monoxide and free oxygen or to form more complex molecules such as Methyl alcohol (CHCCO) I suspect the latter option is probably the best for the home user. Generating hydrogen and oxygen in the same cell can lead to an explosive mixture and it can be difficult to separate the two gasses. A liquid and a gas is a bit easier to separate. Methanol can be stored overnight in a tank and used in a fuel cell to generate electricity and heat. Used properly it can be an attractive cooking fuel. It's not precisely nonpolluting but a lot less so than petroleum and if generated on site, will eliminate a lot of trucking or piping and attendant power or fuel use.

The mere existence of efficient artificial photosynthesis systems in the lab of course doesn't make the idea viable just yet for practical use. The efficiency of some reactions, ten or more times that of photosynthesis is certainly a drawing card but one wonders exactly what an artificial photosynthetic fuel producing panel would look like. Possibly like a sort of flattened tree, with credit-card-sized leaves connected by capillary tubes to carry away the alcohol? Probably we won't know for a while but I suspect that in time, assuming sophisticated fabbing technology and climbing robots we might very well be able to do leaf replacement and any other necessary maintenance more or less like a tree does.

The artificial tree is an idea which captured the Mind of Professor Freeman J. Dyson (Along with many others of course!) Artificial photosynthesis here on earth, based on the cracking and rearrangement of CO_2 and water which are both fairly abundant most places; especially in conventional household air; is a good starting place because it potentially addresses a common and long-standing problem, that of reliable independent, non-centralized power along with storage of energy. Once we understand how to do that, what else might we learn to do. Perhaps a similar set of reactions might be brought to bear upon rock to separate silicon from oxygen and use the silicon, probably linked with hydrogen, nitrogen and other elements to create an entire host of processes and mechanisms not so much at home here on earth perhaps, but the basis for a new future in space.

What can we do about artificial photosynthesis, the neogreen technology? I'd say at this point it's pretty much a Type Two or special interest issue but the more we can learn about solar cells and electrolytic cracking of water the better for the processing of biomass to fuel and the efficient, nonpolluting household use of them. For those interested in the natural sciences or advanced engineering; were I to start college at this point in my life, I can think of few major areas more fascinating. I'd probably start with an undergraduate background in biophysics then on graduation, see where the research was and choose my graduate program either in chemical engineer, biosystems engineering or possibly a field not yet given a specific designation. What we learn is another way for us to vote in a very personal way because it not only determines what we know but to a goodly degree *what* we become. So where should we go from here?

Recalling that this is a book about social issues as well as technological and ecological ones, we'll spend the next three chapters looking at the whole issue of supporting *everyone* in our culture. This is as valid an aim for our technology, our economy and our political system as any other. We'll start with conventional ideas of social welfare in 6 then in chapters 7 and 8 we'll examine a couple fairly radical notions of how to house and feed everyone. After that we'll venture out into the solar system and beyond to have a look at some possible long term futures for the human race.

Chapter 6.

Social Welfare

The question of how persons who could not earn a living or had insufficient family support should be kept alive--if at all--has been with us since there's been civilization. In ages past the professions of begging and prostitution derived largely from inadequate available resources to feed and house the poor. Over the last couple of centuries churches were deemed to be largely responsible for the maintenance of widows, fatherless families and the disabled. Social work has its roots in the charity working church volunteers, mostly women who dispensed largess along with moral lectures to those on the dole.

Today welfare recipients in America belong generally to one or more of three basic categories:

1 Inter-generational welfare recipients, members of families who've been on government assistance possibly since the 1930s, who grow up with no role-modeling of paid employment and no such expectations for themselves;

2 pregnant women as well as low-income women (or men) with children;

3 Persons with physical, mental, emotional and sometimes chemical difficulties which prevent them from working.

The issues of unemployment, unemployability and non-job-readiness are complex as is the sociology of ghettos and the poor generally, so I'll confine this discussion to what I know best, which happens to be the clients of the public assistance system administered by the Department of Social and Health Service of Central Washington State. This is an essentially agrarian region, though dotted with towns large and small; where many of the local residents have no contact or experience with farm living. Though I know of some families who've been on one or another sort of welfare for perhaps three generations, the number of the truly inter-generational public assistance-accessing families are comparatively rare in this part of Northwestern US. Such poverty seems to result from lack of education, perhaps hereditary learning disability and regional economic circumstances which prevent persons from being able to find employment. I've worked for 19 years with the other two groups.

Persons with physical disabilities, resulting either from injury or chronic disease as well as those with one and often several mental health diagnoses, may well have work histories and may be potentially capable of some kind of work but may lack the education or training to do jobs for which they have the physical and mental capability. Some persons may be expected to recover from their physical or mental difficulties and return to work in a reasonable time. Others with more series, long-term disabilities or some young people who on attaining their majority, are new applicants to the welfare system, may need to be evaluated to determine whether they are truly unable to work or if some sort of education, training, special accommodations or appliances may be helpful in seeking and retaining employment. Those who are found able to potentially work are referred to the Department of Vocational Rehabilitation where one or more counselors work with them to assess what services may help them get into the work-force and if available funding can pay for the necessary education, training or special equipment they may need. (By the way, education is the process of gaining knowledge whereas training is the gaining of skills. I didn't understand the difference until I was most of the way through graduate school in Adult Education.) Persons who are considered permanently disabled are referred to either the Special Supplementary Income (SSI) Program or Special Supplementary Disability Income (SSDI) Program. The difference being that in the former case a person has no significant documented history of paid employment while in the second the person has worked before and benefits are based on previous earned income. These Federal programs are essentially the holy Grail for the long-term welfare recipient and the Social Security system is essentially overwhelmed with applications.

The Federal Government fights most applications as far as possible, hoping to discourage a portion of the applicants, requiring most people to retain the services of an attorney before ever seeing one dollar from a Federal program. Persons who will be disabled for a short time, say three to twelve months thereafter which they can reasonably be expected to regain their health, are given a pittance in monthly cash payments or receive some assistance in maintaining shelter from the local Housing Authority. They also have available to them a fairly good level of medical coverage, which includes mental health counseling if necessary, though generally not dental or optical care. At this point in time, nobody on the disability program really receives sufficient funding to cover basic housing needs though so far, food benefits are about sufficient to keep body and soul together.

Welfare system in America and most other places have been primarily oriented toward women with children. Sometimes fathers with children have accessed the same benefits as mothers though there's generally been more of a stigma attached to being a man on welfare. Until about 1997 in all fifty States there was some sort of program available aimed at providing some maintenance for families with children. The general idea was that by allowing mothers to stay home with their children, said children would have supervision and would more likely stay in school longer and be less likely to get in trouble with the law.

(At this point I'm going to say some things which will be controversial. (I'm giving the warning as I obviously not said anything with which anyone could possibly quarrel previously!!) At some point the federal experts in social services looked at a lot of statistics and case studies from the field and decided that mothers expected to stay at home really weren't providing a lot of supervision for children. The kids were running the streets after school, pretty much like those of mothers who worked. It was also true that mothers who stayed home with their children for eighteen or more years, weren't having much success in supporting themselves after their children grew up till minimal Social Security might kick in to help them during their later years. This was the story as I've heard it and I believe it's true. Whatever the reason, something called Work First was conceived. This meant exactly what it purported to; heads of households with children, on public assistance would be helped to go to work, seek work or prepare for work through education, training, in some cases rehab services.

Under Federal law, all States must administer with federal funding; at least two years of Work First services for income eligible clients who were either pregnant had children under 18 or both. Washington State, being one of the more generous of the fifty, legislated five years of Work First for all eligible clients and their families. These services included food and medical benefits, monthly cash payments and support services to help each client progress toward work readiness and hopefully a job. The motto of the Washington State program was and is "A job, a better job, a better life." Work First is administered under The temporary Assistance to Needy Families, (TANF) program. Like any other group, pregnant women and mothers included persons with physical, mental or emotional issues which prevent them from going to work now and possibly for the rest of their lives. These people are referred to the SS/DI process and receive State welfare benefits until a determination can be made on their federal cases.

I liked Work First quite a bit and still do actually but it has a lot of problems. I liked it because though initiated under the Clinton Administration, it came originally out of the more enlightened conservative thinking of the Sixties and Seventies. The somewhat knee-jerk notion that those who did not work should not eat, seemed rather unreasonable in a land where there is really still a great deal of conspicuous wealth, not to mention a lot of boondoggle Federal spending. Still it rankled lots of folks that able-bodied people were perceived to be sitting around on welfare while others had to work. Some people either couldn't find work and women in later stages of pregnancy or caring for small children were at a disadvantage. So, some assistance from county, state or Federal funds in order to keep themselves and their families healthy and reasonably secure appeared to be indicated. Fine, the thinking went, provide the needy person with a subsistence income but let them do something in order to earn the funds allotted. Some felt that welfare recipients should put in time doing volunteer work, some that they should enroll in school or training programs to make themselves more employable. Some even suggested that such persons should at least have to report every work day to a center or facility of some kind, where they'd spend eight hours away from home and television. Work First offered some of the best of this thinking (in my opinion). Women or men on the program could receive vouchers to buy work clothing, get haircuts, have tattoos removed, buy diapers for young children, pay for fuel or receive bus cards to get back and forth to work. Significant subsidies were available for child-care. If a person wasn't currently ready to work because of a lack of experience, skills or basic education, programs were available for completion of high school or GED. A year or more of college or vocational training might be available. There was also a program which essentially handed a person a job part-time and temporary, but paid with 50 percent of her time left open to do job search or further education.

Those able to undertake job search immediately were supported with workshops on interviewing, resume writing and basic life skills as well as a computer database listing jobs, many of them published only for Work First clients. Businesses and agencies in the area were enlisted to make special efforts to hire Work First clients. The intent of the program and I think, generally the practice was to encourage clients to think of themselves not as persons destined to spend their lives relying upon a government subsidy, but rather as able near-future participants in the job market.

The problems were numerous. The effort to find jobs which could be made available to Work First participants were never sufficiently successful and many of those there were had pay-levels so low as to keep the new employees on welfare medical benefits. The five-year TANF benefits limit strictly decreed by the Department of Social and Health Services and used by social workers and case managers to exhort clients to hurry up and get employable before the sixty months ran out, was at the eleventh hour, extended without any end date until the midst of the recession of 2007-8 when they were (again without warning) discontinued for persons who'd received sixty or more months. This lost a great deal of credibility for those of us working day on day with clients.

Much of the money which was earmarked for the TANF program and which was perceived by the general public as taxes going directly to welfare recipients; were in fact paid to medical clinics for various sorts of evaluations, administrative study and policy groups of various kinds and instructors who frequently trained and retrained agency employees in various aspects of counseling, self discovery and office behavior.

These were generally touted as skill-building workshops to help employees more effectively serve clients. Trainings were often devoted to things like learning one's own personality type, learning to redefine what respect meant, or how to direct conversations to get the client to be compliant with program goals. Though not necessarily bad in and of themselves, these workshops generally were licensed study courses developed at places such as The Harvard School of Business Management, which took a great deal of welfare funding and put it in the pockets of social research firms and marketers.

Perhaps the greatest problem of the TANF process was that though some clients grabbed hold of Work First as a means of getting employed, out of poverty and successful in a career, the majority appeared to have no particular interest in going to work and in a great many cases, used any delay they could think of to avoid seeking a job, completing school or doing much of anything else. Even the threat of Sanction, meaning a portion of the client's cash allotment would be taken away and possibly a Protective Payee imposed to oversee the expending those funds left, didn't seem to motivate many persons. Many people ran through their sixty months of TANF with little or nothing to show for it.

Regarding pregnancy programs and benefits for families with young children, it has to be admitted that whether one is working outside the home or not; there's already work enough to do every day and often enough, all day. It's not real surprising that people who've often grown up thinking that welfare existed for people just because they were pregnant or caring for a child, will be resistant when now informed that welfare is something that one needs in a sense to earn, through some sort of participation. Many of the TANF clients are young women and men with little or no employment experience and frankly, a strong sense of social entitlement. Others had problems with TANF and Work First because they assumed that education and training meant that they could go entirely through college to a four-year degree. "I've got five years don't I?" Feelings were hurt and ires roused when clients were told that they were limited to perhaps a year of high school completion or college--doing something aimed at a particular job-goal to raise potential chances of being hired salary expectation.

I'm an education advocate but I know that while college classes are useful for enhancing ones work and promotion potential on an existing job and if a person is employable in the first place and all other things being equal, it's probably better to have a degree than not; the mere possession of a two or four-year degree nowise guarantees one will be hired. Another way of saying this is there are some jobs for which you won't get hired without some sort of degree, but just having the degree doesn't mean you'll be hired for that job or any other.

For one thing the job market is so unstable that it's difficult to know in your freshman year what sorts of job openings will exist when you've graduated. Also, though college is an excellent way to increase your breadth and depth of knowledge, a given degree program needn't teach you to actually *do* anything except write term papers, do library research, solve equations, follow lab manuals. After graduation your first order of business is to convince some employer you're of worth spending time on train you to do a given job. The fact a person is on welfare is evidence that some sort of problem exists with that person's employability. It's not necessarily an insuperable problem but in most cases, professional/technical training aimed at a given skill set and a specific set of jobs known to be available within one's near vicinity, as well as some sort of directed work experience is probably the best strategy for landing a long-term job. That's after all, the whole point of Work First.

So from my somewhat jaundiced perspective, how could welfare programs be improved? I still believe that Work First is essentially a good idea but I don't think it works for most welfare clients. There is a significant minority who take good advantage of the services and programs under the Work First umbrella and do very impressive things. I'd say about 20-30 percent fall within this category. They need some support and maybe some skills acquisition, perhaps some tools and they can make it off TANF in one or two years, maybe less.

The majority of clients who may have aspirations but little ambition, will burn through all their time on the program and may well end up back in the same situation that put them on welfare in the first place. I believe we should and can provide support for pregnant women during the last trimester of their pregnancies and at least three months following delivery without requirement of work or work-prep activities. I don't have a problem with every woman being eligible for sixty months of TANF coverage throughout her life. I also believe that within the first year of TANF benefits we can determine which clients are likely to follow through with a work-readiness program and which are not. For those who are candidates for Work First, I'd keep the program as described above, intact. For those otherwise disposed, I'd withdraw job search or work support services and place them on a program which provides food, housing and a moderate degree of essential needs, clothing, hygiene, medical and transportation services for medical appointments. Food, housings and similar services would be handled by direct payment to vendors or through a voucher system. Cash payments as such would not be made though I'd be generous in allowing the individual client to retain a portion of any money earned through jobs she or her partner/spouse earns on their own. Perhaps most or all benefits would be withdrawn when family earned income reaches 150 percent of the comparable value of benefits received. I'd also withhold all benefits if documentation of earnings is not forthcoming or can be shown to be fraudulent. I'd allow clients in this voucher-based program to transition back into Work First if they request and sign a contract of re-participation and follow through with their program for a reasonable period of time, say 90 days.

It's true that one of the aims of Work First was to limit the number of months any person remained on welfare but I think I've given some evidence that a great deal of the money allocated for welfare benefits never truly reaches the client so I suspect that sustaining a client throughout life wouldn't cost as much as TANF allocations for that same client for five years. We also recall that food, housing, clothing and medical benefits pay wages, taxes and generally help keep the economy functioning.

For clients who do not have children but have disability issues such as physical or mental health; there is a need to provide food and shelter but cash is problematic. I've often observed that persons report themselves as being homeless as well as disabled in an effort to try to force the welfare agency to provide them with monthly income. A great many of the people I've met who report themselves as homeless are in actuality doing what is called couch surfing, staying with various friends and relatives which is not optimum but not exactly sleeping in the park either. One State program for persons with disabilities is currently the HEN (Housing and Essential Needs) program. Clients tend to be very unhappy when told they've been assigned to this particular program because they want cash. In my opinion a person who truly has a disability needs food, shelter and possibly medical or mental health services.

I say *possibly* concerning the medical or mental health services because applicants who are approved for the various disability programs have a rather startling record of not following through with medical or mental health services and keeping such benefits open costs the State or Federal Government a great deal of money. If income eligible medical coverage is available with Federal support then it is available to any welfare client. If such programs are not currently available I think each welfare client on a disability-type program should receive medical coverage from the State for a limited time, perhaps three months, and if they do not follow through, I wouldn't necessarily take away housing and food benefits but I'd let the medical coverage lapse.

In addition on the theory that few people are truly Totally Disabled, I would provide an incentive program which would pay the client in addition to housing and food support and perhaps medical; a stipend for enrolling in a vocational rehabilitation program to be trained to do a job or jobs for which the client is currently capable or is likely to be within six months. The desire for cash might lend ambition to some folks who are on disability not because they are entirely unable to work, but have never done desk work for instance, or customer service, or worked with a computer.

Beyond persons who are currently or recently pregnant and those with disabilities, how should we view welfare for persons who haven't sufficient job skills or who just aren't able to find a job? The frequently voiced notion that there's lots of work out there to be done and unemployed workers could just be put to work cleaning parks, repairing roads, picking up garbage, etc, is a problematic one. There is indeed work out there needing to be done but unions and the court system largely control when and how these sorts of jobs are done. There's also the small issue of funding the administration of any such work program and paying the wages for the workers themselves. Under our present economic system the activities carried out by the reemployed workers, must show some social or financial value for the city, county, state or nation.

During the 1930s surplus apples were sold on street corners by formerly unemployed men and women, providing some residual profit to the farmer and income for the vendors as well as wholesome lunch additions for town and city workers. Programs in broom making, chair re-caning and piano tuning have been set up to train and employ the blind. With the increasing number of women with small children going to work, a notable number of welfare clients have established themselves as child-care providers. With the national population going up again and the number of available jobs decreasing, the prospect of providing work for the generally fit but chronically unemployed person seems bleak under the current business model. The next two chapters deal with some more radical concepts for providing a reasonable degree of income for virtually everyone. Before leaving the topic of social welfare as it exists today however, let us examine what might be done under the present socioeconomic system to provide employment for those who have none.

In order not to interfere with existing livelihoods and penal policies, we can state again that the best way to create new wealth is by taking advantage of a surplus or presently unused resource to satisfy a need which currently goes wanting. So, what do we have of which there's surplus?

We have an overabundance of trash. Landfill refuse is largely claimed by sanitation service departments which tend to be unionized and recyclable materials go in large part to recycling centers. Recyclers are fairly happy with glass, aluminum and paper but plastics continue to be a headache. Some plastics are easily recycled, others aren't, and the non-recyclable sorts such as the thermal-setting variety, (see last chapter) have little residual value. There's also a lot of carbon dioxide in our air which likely shouldn't be. In urban areas there's a lot of animal waste from pets and strays and much of this goes unclaimed. There are also a great number of obsolete or malfunctioning personal computers, phones and other electronic devices generated ever year. Doubtless there are many other sources of largely non-claimed resources but here's a representative sample, so let's take a look at the needs side of the balance ledger.

We need a lot of things but if the need is great enough there is usually a supplier of some type already and at some price. The following isn't meant to be a definitive response to this question merely a suggestion which is illustrative. We continue to build houses, apartments and other living structures requiring materials which are themselves becoming more expensive and difficult to procure. Lumber, for instance purchased at the local home improvement store is of notably poorer quality than it was two or three decades ago. Also since lumber is generally sold as boards of essentially long rectangular shape, which need to be sawn and drilled in various ways to follow some contours and fit into frameworks the idea of made-to-order boards and panels presents itself. Such members could be tongue and grooved and suitably shaped to fill in the wall areas beneath sloped or peaked roofs. These wouldn't need to be of high structural strength, not being particularly load bearing. They could save labor and therefore help hold construction costs down.

How could such board or panel members be created with cost saving and employing persons who may often have limited skills? An answer is suggested by a type of 3-D printer which was almost marketed a few years ago. It used as its build material a finely ground fiber comprised of iron, glass and nylon plastic. Melted together the powder could form into fairly strong items. We therefore need to literally grind up computers, monitors, cell phones, television sets along with unwanted waste plastic gathered by recycling facilities. We'd basically want a source of non-thermal-setting plastic to glue together the powder. Then, a special sort of 3-D printer, looking somewhat like a little railroad track with a little car provided with laser or halogen light source to melt the layers of material. Any length and end-angle of board could be made on demand.

For a source of the plastic with which to glue the powder into a rigid composite we might look at the afore-mentioned animal waste. Dog poop, like most other organic materials, can be made into biodiesel with the addition of some potassium or sodium, some methyl alcohol and moderate heat. If we can make biodiesel we can synthesize plastic. Suddenly we've created a plethora of jobs from animal droppings gatherers and loaders of electronic appliances to machine operators to chemical reactor operators to repair persons to sales and marketing personnel. A little something for everybody. We haven't used much of the carbon dioxide in the air but there are ways of gathering that and including it in certain kinds of insulation material. As we've said this is not intended as an entire answer to the problem of abled unemployment but we will need something like this if we wish to provide a reasonable level of health and comfort for all of our citizens. Having at least postulated this new employment program we need to ask the basic question germane to all current welfare discussions; how do we keep ineligible persons from benefiting? A great deal of the work associated with enrolling clients in welfare programs has to do with initial background checking and ongoing follow-up to determine as well as possible, what each person or family's financial situation actually is. In this case persons claiming not to be employed or able to find a job would seemingly need to show they didn't have a job. It's a little hard to see why someone already employed adequately would seek another job. We're assuming these salaries won't be overly generous but eventually someone will figure out some nefarious reason for someone to seek a Created Job. I suppose some number of signed notes from local employers indicating that jobs have been applied for and the applicant rejected, perhaps twenty--might suffice as evidence of unemployability. Evidence of a minimal bank balance for a period of time might be another. In the end does it make a difference if someone takes a created job meant for persons who'd otherwise be on welfare because isn't some other job potentially left open?

Now let's go a bit further afield to take a more basic look first at the economy then our technology. In the next chapter we'll consider Universal Credit, the handing out of surplus money to the needy (or to everyone) as a means of balancing the economic system. In Chapter 8. We'll examine a concept for restructuring the concepts of livelihood and human needs support.

Chapter 7.

Universal credit payments

This is an economic concept which goes at least back to the 1930s and was advocated by Upton Sinclair who ran for Congress and also for governor of California. The idea is explained in Robert A. Heinlein's first novel "For Us The Living" which he subsequently secreted away and it wasn't published until after the deaths of Robert and his wife, Virginia. Universal credit, though essentially economic, is also ecological in a sense because though it is socialistic in nature, it's more about balance than welfare. We'll take an ecological example to serve as analogy through which to look at universal credit. Using our spaceship model let's say that we've got a solar greenhouse in which we can grow some grains, some legumes, some greens, some berries or other fruit; in short all of the necessities of a balanced diet. We recycle our water, condensing it out of the air of the greenhouse for drinking, cooking bathing. What is called gray water is added to growing beds to water the plants. For our metabolic output we have toilets which feed into an anaerobic digester which turns what we put out into methane gas and a rich source of liquid fertilizer. This goes back to the greenhouse and the plants.

We'll also point out that as plants can't make vitamin B which is essential for human health, we include some chickens or pond fish in our system. Also the methane and carbon dioxide which comes from the digester needs to be cycled back to the greenhouse. The methane burns to complete the water cycle and the CO2 returns to the plants to complete the carbon cycle. The liquid effluent itself needs some exposure to oxygen in order to become useful to the plants as fertilizer. The greenhouse plants which require nitrogen from their soil must be balanced with those which deposit nitrogen and the various types of proteins making up our nutritional needs must be balanced as well in terms of crops planted and harvested.

Now as we've inferred, if we don't burn the methane from our digester, the greenhouse will lack some of the water and carbon dioxide it needs. If we don't consume all of the plants matter produced in one way or another at an appropriate rate, the plants will lack for carbon dioxide, water and trace minerals. If plants lack any of these things, food production will drop and we'll have less to eat. If we eat less, the cycle will spiral downward. If some faction among our spaceship's crew should claim sole ownership of the food supply, the only way the rest of the crew could feed themselves short of violence, would be to find something the hoarders might value which could be traded for a share of the ship's provisions. Obviously if the majority of the crew wasn't able to eat, soon enough everyone would be experiencing famine because of the overall cycle decaying or halting altogether. The ecosystem could be shrunk to match the size of the hoarding minority but for everyone else, illness, starvation, almost certainly revolution must ensue, probably not in that order!

Whether or not the dispossessed portion of the crew has anything to give back to the food growers, the only way to keep the entire ship viable is to find some way of equitably distributing rations to everyone. This being done we again have a work-ready crew who can attend to the other ship functions such as navigation, propulsion and repair. There may be hobbies and useful skills which can provide additional services to everyone; guitar-playing for instance, teaching, counseling, cooking, beer-making. You get the idea.

It's sort of fascinating that in a small community such as a village or a colony of pilgrims the solutions to basic problems of existence are fairly obvious. Everybody needs some subsistence level of nutrition, clothing and other things. Everybody needs to pitch in what they can and not everyone will pitch in the same things or amounts or for that matter consume at the same rate. When we're looking at the nation or heaven forbid the planet, things are a lot different. What we've been talking about is a potential communist revolution in the making and though it's now not politically correct to pick on communists, those of us who are over on the conservative side still aren't real happy about communism.

Let's build an economic model to see if we can find some kind of basis upon which most of us can agree. First let's say we've got a number of farms each worked by hand or with the aid of a horse. Each farm more or less provides enough food to feed the farm husband and wife, children and the horse. The more or less is crucial because if it's more then there might but a little extra to pay the local blacksmith when a plough, hoe or wagon-wheel breaks; the herbalist who treats injuries, illnesses and delivers babies, the priest who accepts tithes and distributes some of them to destitute widows, orphaned children or persons whose farms have failed. Perhaps there'll be a few other specialists, not too many. Everybody works pretty much from dawn to dusk to earn approximately what he or she needs to survive. Of course besides church tithes there always seem to be land taxes, tribute for armies passing through, or the third portion due to the lord of the manor, but we're keeping things simple.

Now let's say mechanization has set in. Farmers can cultivate much larger holdings and there are fewer of them. The blacksmith has given way to the farm equipment manufacturing corporation, the local midwife has given way to the county hospital. The church in most cases is no longer the community welfare agency but it still wants its ten percent. Of course taxes now exist and mostly get collected.

Besides this we have a higher level of expectation as to what we use and expect to buy, home appliances, entertainment devices, personal transport vehicles, lots of clothing, college tuition, medical insurance, on and on. Now let's say Farmer A needs a new tractor. He probably doesn't have the cash needed in his pocket so he could go to all the various people who buy his produce or perhaps to the stores which act as outlets for him and try to work a lot of small loans but crops are also available from Farmer B and she might very well cut her own profit margin just to push A out of business. A therefore goes to a bank and arranges a loan which ultimately will be paid back with money A will earn selling his crops over the next few years. Farmer A can now go to the FEMC and order his tractor. Productivity will increase--hopefully.

Now let's say that the ACME Shirtwaist company over in town which has been providing blouses to half the State suddenly fails, putting two hundred skilled but rather specialized workers out of a job. Savings in the local bank are withdrawn, sales at the local grocery go down. Less produce is required from Farmers A and B. Perhaps A won't be able to make his loan payments and he loses not only his tractor but his farm. B moves into a better spot economically until she needs some new equipment, at which time the bank may not have sufficient funds to accommodate her.

Again, this is a simplistic model and in such situations what may happen is some kind of assistance from a State or Federal government may be available. We call this either unemployment insurance or welfare. Money flows back, if somewhat sparingly, into the pockets of laid-off workers and the system strikes a new balance, more or less.

As we observed with our spaceship example, carbon dioxide, water, nitrogen and trace minerals must continuously be swapped back and forth between plants and animals (including crew) if anything is going to work properly. For the economy, cash (shorthand for goods and services) plays the role of water and respiratory gases. If a business fails, the effect resounds through everyone. Even if most of the workers never dealt with a local bank, the bank will still be affected because of the farmer's inability to sell his crops and make her payments. The FEMC may not sell a combine next year. Its well-trained, high-paid employees may feel a drop in wages. Medical insurance premiums will go unpaid. People may move elsewhere. Schools may close. Just as in our space ecology where we must burn methane whether we really need it as fuel or not, our economy may need cash infusions at various places in order to stay reasonably balanced. Surely we can look to other communities to absorb our dispossessed workers, and to other farmers and other stores to supply our food needs, but what if, when looking at the entire economy of the world, there continue to be imbalances?

A basic rule of economics is that the money in circulation must equal the value of goods and services available in the market place. This is kind of another way of saying if there's not enough money to buy all the stuff in the store then some stuff won't be sold. Of course prices can be dropped to bring in whatever money the store can, but then wages tend to drop and less money is available for store employees to buy shirtwaists and rototillers and lottery tickets. If there's too much money around then prices tend to rise, making everything cost more. Add to this state of affairs that with increased automation the number of jobs available is shrinking and many of those still available require somewhat arduous and expensive training or education. The people who operate the factories and own the big machines are in the same position as the food hoarders in our spaceship. If they can't sell their output they can't pay their technical staff, nor the janitorial and lunchroom workers. Nor can the company owners enjoy the ambient life support system we call economy; which depends on everyone having enough to eat, wear and live within so those who can provide goods and services can continue to do so. No matter how wealthy an industrialist may be, she or he depends for a good deal of life satisfaction upon gas station attendants, wait staff, drycleaners and sales clerks who may be earning quite modest wages.

It's the folks who can't seem to provide goods or services sufficient to keep body and soul together who are the sticking point. 'Those who don't work shouldn't eat' is a very old and not entirely ill-founded maxim but consider the following. One person sits and sorts beans by size, color, degree of brokenness, texture of skin. Another person sits all day and decides what sort of pretty pictures should go on toothpaste boxes and soap wrappers. One of these people we call an ad exec or at least a commercial artist and pay a pretty high salary. The other person we call a, well, bean sorter and when asked what salary that person should receive we say "What?" Now who really gives a damn what sorts of advertising goes on our toothpaste or tampon box or disposable diaper pack? Oh yeah, Advertisers, a Special Interest Type Two Issue! On the other hand, there might well be a use for the service the other person is providing, especially if some of the work can be mechanized. Something like this happened in C. S. Forrester's lesser-known novel, Randall and the River of Time. The point is, we spend all kinds of money on activities which are calculated to manipulate people to make one choice or other but we balk at spending a comparatively small percentage of our GNP to balance the economy.

How would such Balancing Payments be made? To work properly, I believe the money needs to be in circulation and probably shouldn't be put away as long-term investments or put to some other activity that would generate interest. Perhaps the checks or coupons or E-currency should be timed so if not used within, say, thirty days, it goes away and if the serial number of a given credit allotment doesn't show within that time, the credit can be awarded again later. Some people will get some surprises now and again and that could be handled as a sort of cost-free lottery. Everyone should be included because the credits shouldn't be so generous as to remove all incentive to work (if that's really a huge issue), but might be generous enough to allow a low-income person to live at least at some moderate level of health and safety. It may not actually be the best idea to just hand out money or credit.

Though I'm not sure that bean-sorting is the best thing to ask everybody to do, there might be several activities of fairly low impact and some social value which could be performed in return for this basic subsidy payment received because we're citizens or even just residents. I'm thinking of a state computer game, a simulated market, place which could generate interesting psychological and socioeconomic data and might be of use to the toothpaste artists. Another might be writing alternative segments to enormous choose your own adventure novels. Lots of people want to be writers and it's not as if anyone is forced to read them. Of course there is also reading to patients in hospitals, telling stories to kids in the public library, taking a disabled person shopping, whatever.

Is this something as individuals we can do anything about? Sure.
It affects us. It certainly shouldn't be imposed on us without a
vote so it's a matter for the polls, IE, a Type Three issue. Can we
do anything about getting it instituted? At least one State has put
it up for a vote. Sound out your gubernatorial candidates. We
could cut welfare spending, maximize employment (the old-
fashioned kind), and keep our market more stable. Something for
everybody!

Chapter 8.

Autopreponderance

A Rational Independence

In the early days of The United States visionaries who looked toward America's future differed with one another in a fundamental way. The Jeffersonians wanted to keep things essentially local and fairly small. Thomas Jefferson wrote that the best sort of man was the farmer on his own land. Most of the things needed to sustain life could be had from a reasonably-sized land-holding and a lot of hard work. Of Course Jefferson never lived on the sort of farm obtainable by the average family in 1800 and he was awash with expensive imports from Europe so his personal economy depended upon sufficient wealth to reach beyond the local agrarianism to a decidedly non-Jeffersonian system of industry abroad. Hamiltonians looked to strong central rule to regulate and protect trade. A powerful federal government would raise armies, float navies, provide a legal and economic framework for factories and businesses to develop, grow and flourish. The first two United States presidents were essentially Hamiltonians.

George Washington lived much like Jefferson when he could be at home but was fairly congruent with Hamilton's political and economic views because he invested in a variety of far-reaching enterprises, including mule-breeding, whiskey-making systems of canals and an early attempt at building a steamboat. John Adams was never as economically successful as either Washington or Jefferson but he shared the view of a centralized, business oriented culture for the new nation. Up until about 1860 the majority of US   presidents were largely of the Jeffersonian viewpoint and though America now operates much more on a Hamiltonian model than a Jeffersonian; we still call up the Jeffersonian ideals when we celebrate our culture. The individual is still seen at least emotionally, as the basic unit of American society and many city-dwellers harbor a nostalgia for life on the farm even if they've never lived on one. Farm fresh, rural living, raw milk, farmer's market, range fed, bread basket of America are all for many of us, phrases with which to conjure.

When I was in college, carrying an engineering major and a strong minor in editorial journalism, I was irked by the general assumption that the future portended increasing specialization and the increasing dominance of large corporations over small ones and individual entrepreneurships. I wrote in a term paper at one point that a basically Jeffersonian system of living was still possible through scientific farming methods and alternative energy technology. I don't recall what my professor commented on that point if at all but lots of people must have agreed with me. Around that time a significant back-to the-land movement was underway, extolled and chronicled by a Magazine called The Mother Earth News, which in large measure gave its name to the social trend it reported. 'Mother,' as she was affectionately called by her devotees, largely began reporting the old ways of doing things, making soap, grinding grain, organic gardening, operating your own well, building windmills.

Fairly soon though things started appearing that most people didn't know about such things as fermenting slurries of manure, water and other organic matter to generate methane-containing biogas, or building your own solar panels. Mother also devoted a lot of space to advice on how to acquire land, build your own or make use of per-existing houses, cabins, barns, sheds; along with accounts of those who'd successfully done these things. Phrases like cash poor, land-rich and living off the grid acquired a certain panache among aspiring homesteaders, hobby and subsistence farmers.

I spent a great deal of time in college and thereafter, thinking about the basic wherewithal for a person or family to be independent upon a few acres of land, anywhere--even on an asteroid. There must be commonalities. I tried to decide what really constituted independence. On a farm here on Earth we would take air for granted and we wouldn't be farming at all without some source of water and we mustn't forget soil. On an asteroid we'd assume sunlight as well as the rock itself so no matter what else was true, we'd have to assume these things upon which we must depend. Assuming these things then, what capabilities must we have in order to be considered independent? Growing all or most of our food would be a requirement certainly as well as generating our power from sources either on our land, such as wind and water or which we contrive, such as solar water heaters, alcohol fuel, methane gas or a wood lot. Beyond this, what? Must we be able to build our machines? If so, must we know how to smelt metal and forge tools, cast replacement parts? Must we make all of our own clothes? Medications? Grooming and hygiene products? Laura Ingalls Wilder rhapsodized about all the things Pa and Ma made throughout the year but even Ma bought cloth and flour and Pa must buy gunpowder, fiddle strings, and all of his tools. Meanwhile our ambient culture was telling us that monetary self-reliance was the primary goal of one's working life and what made the economy and the world go 'round.

I'd been out of college for perhaps five years when I visualized a house/farmstead system which could be constructed, if not by a single person, at least by a network of members with specialized training and tools; each member turning out finished items such as an engine a wood stove or a refrigerator, beginning with recycled materials and proceeding to a working appliance. In a manner similar to Habitat for Humanity, of which I'd not heard yet in those days; a person would be set up with a house, a basic energy generating system and the wherewithal to farm three to ten acres. Once so equipped and entitled the new member would devote a certain number of hours per year helping to produce items needed by newer members and replacement parts for broken or malfunctioning devices and systems. Of course not everyone would have the same range of skills or access to tools. I wasn't requiring my members to build their own cars, though a Stirling-type generator system seemed reasonable.

I called my micro-tech network concept "Autopreponderance" meaning that one was largely independent assuming the network had as a given the presence of air, water, soil and sunlight. I wrote the first of several drafts of a book which bore the same title as this chapter around 1983.

Autopreponderance employs specialization but is based upon localized systems rather than extensive utility grids so though breakdowns will likely happen much more often, there are a lot of working homesteads around, which hopefully will under the good-neighbor ethic, help one another out if a water pump fails for instance.

As a participating member each person would be entitled to any replacement parts, or even systems such as generators or refrigerators that they needed. The autopreponderant network would also function as a sort of safety net for the overall society. Should the Conventional Technology fail for some reason such as an attack by an electromagnetic pulse weapon (a prospect which is frighteningly plausible) I assumed that there would still remain the modern highly interdependent and specialized technology, but the Autopreponderancy would form a segment of society like agribusiness or public services. It would be an option, an alternative, for folks who wished a greater degree of control in their lives and over the processes which sustained them. Even persons with certain disabilities, social issues or gender conflicts could live a reasonably comfortable existence without having to deal with bosses or customers.

So how realistic is the Autopreponderant Network? In most of the Continental United States we'd need to grow our winter fuel supply. For that, about three dry tons of dry biomass is needed, probably from trees or grass. About four acres of tree lot would be needed to produce enough new wood to satisfy this requirement. Some grasses can provide the same amount of stored energy from considerably less area. To this we must add at least an acre of "good farmland" on which to raise food for a family of four. If animals are used for ploughing and other agricultural processes, more arable land for grain and root crops would be needed. Of course we'd need a well or a creek to supply water. Five acres and independence is about right.

Efficient solar absorbers can be made from flame-blackened copper sheeting, concentrating reflectors can be made from aluminum sheets. Both materials are potentially recyclable if a bit troublesome to regenerate as thin, uniform sheeting. Solar cells are useful, especially in the summer for producing electricity. They can be made by depositing thin layers of silicon dioxide (sand) with some additives, along with delicate traceries of conductive copper on a metal surface. Windmills can be made by hand or automatically, from wood and some fairly simple mechanical components machined from steel or aluminum.

Refrigerators and even air conditioners can be based on processes employing ammonia/water solutions or desiccants, and driven by heat.

Assuming a winter fuel supply and a burner of some kind, a 6,000-pound mass of fuel burned over an 180-day period gives us an average heat flow of 17,300 BTUs per hour, sixteen hours per day. That's about four point eight kilowatts. Now if we're burning that much fuel (approximately two pounds per hour) we're well-advised to consider using our fuel in an engine to generate mechanical work or electricity as well as heat. This lets our heat energy provide lighting and other fairly sophisticated functions on its way to warming us. If concentrated summer sunlight can replace winter heating fuel to continue the supply around the calendar, so much the better. Electrical lighting, the motion of fans, cooking functions will all end up ultimately as heat in our living space.

Small engines tend to convert heat to mechanical motion with low efficiency. A steam engine or air-type engine such as a Stirling cycle fed by a continuous supply of pelletized grass might possibly convert fifteen percent of its fuel's energy into mechanical work. That means that our four point eight kilowatts of winter heat might furnish as much as 700 watts of mechanical power which can in turn be converted at fairly high efficiency to electricity. This is optimistic but in the ballpark for small gasoline engines so clever design might achieve the same efficiency for alternatively powered generators. Engines radiate heat due to combustion so the radiator of our engine will be our primary household heater. Assuming such an engine therefore, can we build it in what would amount to a garage or basement workshop?

The bottle-neck of the entire autopreponderant process really appears to be the precision of mechanical parts we can produce in a small facility. At the time of my first draft about the closest we'd come to what we'd later call desktop manufacturing was a process whereby a pair of lasers could cause points in a transparent plastic material to become opaque. The material which remained transparent could then be machined away and the opaque portion used as a positive mound from which a negative could be made with sand or plaster and molten metal used to reproduce the original opaque shape. Since that time of course, numerous systems have been developed for making metal parts from powder or filaments of one sort or another. Such 3-D fabbing systems can also make a good many of their own parts with the notable exception of the laser or electron beam needed to melt the metal feed stock and build up the component desired. Such systems are quite expensive but once purchased can allow us to turn out any number of engines part by part.

If we can make an engine, we can make compressors, refrigerators, pelletizers, rototillers, electric motors, generators and well pumps. CO_2 lasers and similar high-energy devices have been built in home shops or school laboratories, but generally using a lot of off-the-shelf parts. Whether or not the autopreponderancy must trade heat engines for instance with the traditional technological sector for lasers remains to be seen Sophisticated glass production would need to be added to the network's wherewithal, besides the capability of making coils and circuits, necessary for building electric motors and generators. It's been proposed that on the moon for instance, beams of highly-concentrated sunlight might be used for selective laser sintering. Such beams with lower intensity of course, have been used for such things as optic surgery in third-world nations though in America the intensity of sunlight needed may not be up to the manufacturing demands of a fair-sized community.

Beyond the laser there is a more mundane lighting issue that of common household illumination. I'm sure any community with a glass furnace and a skilled glass blower could reproduce incandescent bulbs. Fluorescent coils would be harder to make, probably requiring the ability to extrude glass tubing and it might turn out to be just more reasonable to buy such things as bulbs due to their relative cheapness but a colony on Mars may well need to fabricate their own lighting systems along with most of the other things they use because resupply missions from Earth will be seldom and slow in coming. Obviously, any reasonably developed country has a technology of sufficient sophistication to make both light bulbs and laser emitters but how "small" can a community become while yet retaining the complexity to fabricate electrical and optical components? As an illustration let's look at a possible light-bulb-making process.

The lightbulb fabricator would begin with recyclable glass for most operations but would know how to formulate anew if necessary. The fabricator would also know how to build and operate a small glass furnace, how to blow glass, possibly using negative molds and would be able to fabricate the bulb filaments, probably using a fabber. Broken bulbs would be returned to the "lighting specialist." A laser fabricating operation might work much the same way but with more steps involved. The human fabricator could take advantage of fairly simple robots to assist in materials-handling and assembly. The robots would either rely upon computer brains or old-fashioned mechanical calculators could be made to accept sensor data, do numerical processing and issue orders to robotic arms and other effectors. Everyone might well have some sort of robot along with heat engine, generator, pumps, gardening equipment and kitchen appliances but fabbers would likely be shared within the community and possibly even rented to outsiders in exchange for items not addressed within the network.

If we can manufacture all of the components making up an engine, including pistons, connecting rods, crank shafts, heat exchangers and combustors, what of such things as piping, tanks and metal sheeting? There are basically two methods for making fairly large uniform sheets and pressure vessels at the home workshop level. As with laminated wooden boat hulls, a tank could be built up of thin plies glued up and initially stapled till the glue sets. It is a bit harder to build up a bottle than an open boat hull but we might work with a pneumatic form against which to put up the first layer or a large slug of ice might be used, most likely in the wintertime. The other concept involves woven wire.

In order to fabricate solid metal objects with a 3-D printer we will need either powdered metal or wire. The former can be made by forcing superhot steam or gas to melt metal. The other way is to force molten metal through small holes in a steel or ceramic plate. Wire like most other fibers can be woven into cloth, knitted or braided around a form to create an envelope of a given shape. Once we have a woven sheet or enclosure of wire cloth we can immerse it in an electrolyte solution and electroplate the same or another metal into the cloth to form a continuous, air/water-tight vessel. This is another of those processes such as we discussed a couple chapters back, in which we can set up the operation and run the system when sunlight is available to supply electricity.

Beyond wood-ply and impregnated wire structures it should be noted that polyethylene can be synthesized in comparatively few steps from ethyl alcohol and it is recyclable.

Houses;   These largest component of the autopreponderant network would need to be largely standardized and would probably be best constructed using a series of truss frameworks, comprising supports for floor, walls and roof in each unit. The trusses would be tied together with longitudinal stringers or beams and the whole could be kept weatherproof with repeatable exterior panels, possibly made from doped fabric of some kind, wood plies and plastic or other shapeable composites. Even if an house shell is standardized by the co-op network, niceties such as individualized interiors and custom flooring could be added at the owner's option.

At this point a person might understandably ask what's the point or points actually as there are quite a few. Why should we create this parallel economy within the ambient National economic system/industrial system which requires everyone to start with either a common raw material such as wood or sand or a something recycled such as glass or aluminum and construct a finished product, possibly with moving, electrical or optical parts? Like the afore-mentioned habitat for humanity project, autopreponderance is a way for a person or a family or other grouping to acquire a house and all things pertaining thereto for little or nothing down. Since network members would need to exchange finished products with fair frequency, they'd likely live in near proximity to one another, probably on tracts of land which could be purchased in common. Per acre costs are much lower at the wholesale real estate level and difficult for individuals to acquire. Of course anyone who already owned property could also participate. Though the complexity of some fabrication and assembly processes might appear at first daunting, the actual number of units of any particular item required during a given period might very well be sufficiently low as to leave most of a person's working time free.   Therefore members, though contracted to do a certain amount of work for the network during each year, would have most of their time free to pursue writing, art, charity work, travel or something else they really want to do.

This would be an optimum lifestyle for those with aesthetic temperaments or unsalable college majors, especially since each member would be given training and experience in constructing a tangible, nonperishable, working device or structural member. This is a good deal more than the average factory worker can say under our existing system. By largely avoiding cash and the need for conventional wage or salary employment, the autopreponderancy would be a buffer against the impending imbalance but capital/production and laborer/consumer. It would also be difficult to tax network members because their obligatory working hours would be comparatively few and profit as such would not exist. I guess from my own prospective a major attraction of this kind of system would be to provide an opportunity to work with my hands part of the time without the need to sell anything or even get hired, which would balance the essentially intellectual activities I currently do to earn my salary.

So what's involved in setting up an autopreponderant network? For an initial design study I once did relating to a projected interstellar colony I estimated that an autopreponderant community with a technological capability equaling or surpassing the needs support we require at the present time in the US would require a minimum membership of a thousand participating makers, each working ten to fifteen hours per week. Family farm work would be additional.

I dubbed this thousand worker community with dependents a "Millennium," suggested by the ancient Roman Century of one hundred infantry soldiers. A thousand families each with five acres of land would be able to live on a tract of land about eight square miles in extent; providing that suitable water was available for crops. That's not even an inordinately large plantation by the standards of the Old South. Besides the land involved of course we'd need initial set-up of shops, one or more metal-capable fabbers a system of transport, a computer accounting system and of course, a governing body. Hopefully we would not allow the development of a specialist group of governing personnel but would add administrative duties to the usual membership share. Perhaps everyone would take a turn from time to time at administration rather like jury duty though longer in duration.

One major problem with any labor-based cooperative with a full franchise in remuneration is that of getting each member to put in the requisite amount of time, producing the necessary number of units per month or year. Anyone with outside interests would tend to expend effort in that direction if there was a good chance of showing a monetary profit beyond the network. I think the best way to deal with this issue is to create a sort of network scrip or credit similar to that in the previous chapter, which is time-dependent. A unit of commodity produced on the first day of a given period would be worth more than one produced on the second day and much more than one delivered on the last. The actual rate of devaluation of the network currency could be reevaluated from time to time, hence the computerized accounting. Since the units produced by each worker would be of a nonperishable nature, it would be in the community's best interest to encourage production early in the period though not so early that storage facilities are overloaded with product waiting to be requested. Allocation of units for each member to produce would be statistical. An attempt would be made to assign specialties to new members or perhaps retrain some veterans from time to time but there will inevitably be some imbalance in hours worked per week. On the other hand, one would be guaranteed replacements for everything that fails so we've in effect reinvented Karl Marx's Storehouse or for that matter, that of Robin Hood.

Since everyone will be carrying out a comprehensive series of manufacturing processes each person will be provided hands-on training in getting the chosen job done. Work assignments would be made partly on the basis of past education and experience but temperamental testing would also be brought into play because most of us don't have the sort of education or training required to do all aspects of a given classification. A given assignment might well require elements of chemistry, mechanics, metallurgy, automation and several other disciplines. Standardization however will make the teaching process at least direct and transparent. There are a lot of different specialties available. nearly everyone can accomplish something.

The eight square mile autopreponderant plantation/cooperative still seems a bit grandiose but this is not the only way autopreponderance can be initiated. A cogenerative steam-powered generator able to operate on fuel pellets or concentrated sunlight, producing both electricity or high-speed mechanical work plus hot water for the shower would be of considerable value to rural folks subject to frequent blackouts, vacationers and latter-day back-to-the-landers. A small group of people could collaborate to make systems of this kind, partly from off-the-shelf stock, partly from fabbed components. The group might even invest in grassland which could be harvested for fuel pellet material. If all of the members were supplied thereby with an energy prime mover for their homes, the membership would have enriched everyone by the equivalent of several thousand dollars. Once tooled up and trained, perhaps with some members making heat exchangers, some pistons and piston rings, some fireboxes, some pellet drives, other devices or other systems of devices might be manufactured on a unit by unit basis either for members or to be sold for resources to benefit the group. Little by little the network could expand its membership and range of capabilities. Of course autopreponderant networks could be built up around food, clothing, fabbers, robots, any number of things.

Here on Earth the autopreponderant network offers the possibility for individuals to take a very direct hand in recycling, propagation of renewable energy and a quite flexible alternate lifestyle. In space we'll need to use a shop style of manufacturing such as is employed in Italy because it will be a likely be a long time before sufficient numbers of workers, human or robotic, will be available to undertake the specialized assembly-line processes upon which most first-world economies depend. Autopreponderant technology wouldn't but the system of choice for erecting skyscrapers or suspension bridges but it's up to providing for the needs of a village. It's also portable and can be undertake with a relatively small mass of tools and machinery. Our access to space will for some time be through rather small conveyances. Our shop tools and fabbers can travel where foundries and automotive plants cannot. On other planets among the asteroids and in space habitats, the Autopreponderancey will be the ambient technology.

Chapter 9.

So: What *About* Space?

The general topic of Space exploration has probably been one of the more controversial issues of modern times. The term space or astronautics initially referred to any effort to send craft or other objects beyond the earth's atmosphere. More recently one has needed to define what is meant by Space research and development because most people accept the need in today's world and economy for communication and weather satellites and most people who think seriously about national defense or world peacekeeping will probably at least allow that orbital reconnaissance is a significant component in either effort. Things get a little murkier when we discuss putting human beings beyond the atmosphere, in orbit or on interplanetary trajectories. What can we say about Human space flight, therefore? And will there ever be a time when more of us than just a few astronauts will live and work in space?

I choose not to deal with the debate over whether ours or any other government should be involved in human-crewed space missions. I do think however that commercial space flight though still in a fledgling state; is on its way to eventually superseding government-funded efforts. In this chapter I want to discuss what appears at this point, to be what we might reasonably be able to accomplish in the next century or so: and what advantage if any; these efforts might be to humanity. Arthur C. Clarke (Yes, the author of 2001 a Space Odyssey and *much else!)* said in 'The Promise of Space' that if the rocket as a vehicle for going into space lasts as long as the steam locomotive, he would be very surprised. The steam locomotive lasted about 130 years, from around 1820 to 1949, and we started taking tentative steps into the fringes of space in 1947, so the rocket has at this writing and according to Clarke, less than 70 years remaining. Most reasonable people will agree that one can't make exact estimates as to the obsolescence of any technology but I think that if we are to do significant things in space which involve any very large number of average or nearly average people, Clarke is likely right in saying we'll have something better than rockets as we know them now.

What's wrong with rockets? They expend a great deal of energy. A kilogram of mass, (the size of a big block of cheese) needs to be endowed with 32.4 million joules of energy to be in near-Earth orbit. That's nine kilowatt hours of electricity. The most energy-efficient rocket that is possible to build requires about four times that much energy and most rocket systems require about ten times as much by the time we actually get the payload up there. So that's about 360 kilowatt hours of energy for every kilo of mass orbited. Thirty-six thousand kwh for every ton. Rocket fuel, and liquid oxygen, not to mention the maintenance cost on even a reusable rocket aren't nearly as cheap as utility power either. Rockets operating on the fusion principle (the reaction which powers the sun essentially) will likely someday, be able to put stuff in space for a much lower per pound cost but the ships themselves are likely to be very large and enormously expensive to build.

Things like anti-gravity and antimatter aren't likely to help us along the road to space over the next century or so. Anti-gravity if it's possible, would likely run on electricity or something like it and we'd need to somehow generate that aboard the ship. The amount of energy to get into orbit remains the same and could well increase depending on the efficiency of the hypothetical anti-gravity engine. Antimatter might conceivably power a small relatively inexpensive rocket but we don't seem to have any idea how to generate and store more than a few atoms of the incredibly explosive antimatter at one time. In short, if we're limited to using any kind of rockets for space launches, our passenger list is likely to be filled largely by government-sponsored experts and multi-millionaires.

So if the rocket is so expensive, do we have any prospect of large numbers of people ever living and working in space? I believe so. Space travel will always be an energy expensive proposition but we can likely do better than rockets--if we want to. One notion is an electromagnetic catapult track located on a high mountain range near the equator. The track perhaps forty-fifty miles long, would launch small rocket stages upward and outward to rendezvous with a human-carrying craft, pushing it at bearable accelerations and saving a great deal of fuel. The catapult would use an enormous amount of power but this might be supplied for perhaps five minutes every week or so, if a dedicated city agrees to go on emergency standby power for the brief interval necessary.

A catapult firing comparatively small matter projectiles vertically upward could in a half hour or so endow a craft with sufficient velocity to coast to geosynchronous orbit, the only one possible for a vertically-climbing craft. The projectiles from the catapult might be vaporized by laser energy either from the craft or from the ground to sort of blast the craft along with a hot gas plume. This appears to be about the least energy expensive means of getting into space with a primarily-electric reusable system-- except for possibly the beanstalk. Beanstalks or sky hooks are those forty-two thousand mile long structures a lot of folks want to build in orbit and extend them till they touch the ground or alternately a point just above the atmosphere. I'm not comfortable with anything so huge, long and flexible near my planet. The terrorist opportunities are just too phenomenal!

There are some other ways to get payloads into orbit using mostly electrical power and systems once built will remain in operation for years or decades. As we've been told by Doctor Gerard O'Neil and others, building materials can be catapulted from the moon for a small fraction of the cost of shipping up from Earth and that's true, once we have a working catapult on the moon. Once this happens, even if we are still using rockets down here, we can build either space ferries which are light weight and pack in a lot of passengers or we can build very small personal spacecraft which could be worn more or less like a spacesuit and could be orbited by a smallish missile. In either circumstance, there are ways to build structures rather like the beanstalk which will stay respectfully outside of the atmosphere and by spinning about a center of mass in such a manner as to cancel out orbital velocity with its spin around the short axis, could essentially "whip" spacecraft up to orbital speed. That means that our rockets would only have to leap a couple hundred miles up into the sky which uses only about one tenth of the energy of getting into orbit. Basically then we need a base on the moon and the wherewithal to build a catapult and until we have that, we'll be stuck with the egghead and billionaire spacegoing manifest.

So what are the chances of building a base on the moon and if we do that, where does that get us in the solar system?

Technology exists for extracting oxygen from lunar soil or regolith. There appears to be water on the moon and water can be recycled in a number of ways. In the initial stages of any lunar base or settlement food will need to be imported, in freeze-dried form or as dried grain and legumes from Earth. One Apollo-sized mission per year could supply the food needs of a dozen people. Basically we can have a moon base if we are willing to fund (somehow) a Saturn V. or comparable carrying capacity every year. If the outpost can be made to pay for itself in some way, it would expand and eventually food could be grown locally, perhaps not meeting all of the needs of colonists though this would be the goal, but the bulk of food could be grown under domes or with grow lights within caves or bunkers.

The best way for the moon to pay for itself appears to be by dropping material into earth orbit where it can be processed into building material and fuel. With the use of robotic devices and fabricators lunar personnel could conceivably refine lunar materials to extract iron, aluminum and other metals, sufficient to build a catapult or mass driver, able to launch perhaps a kilogram of mass at a given time, to Lunar escape velocity. This would require about three megawatts of power which in turn would need about thirty thousand square meters of solar collectors to power it. That's seven and a half acres of solar cells. A pretty big starting cost but such a project might be possible using machines which can copy themselves (See Chapter 4) and a somewhat lengthy start-up time.

Would a kilogram payload of mass thrown into orbit around Earth be of any use? Not by itself probably but if we could do this every minute perhaps, it would put most of a ton in earth orbit over a 24-hour period.

So what's so special about a bunch of rock in earth orbit? For one thing, 46 percent of aluminum oxide is oxygen. Silica or common sand, (also common on the moon) is 53 percent oxygen. Oxygen obviously can be breathed and can be liquefied as an oxidizer for rockets. A stockpile of liquid oxygen in near earth orbit would greatly simplify missions from earth to higher orbits, the moon or other planets. It would only be necessary to boost rocket fuel into orbit, kerosene for instance or liquid methane, refill oxygen tanks and proceed.

It's possible to use powdered aluminum for fuel in something called a hybrid rocket. Silicon can be combined with hydrogen to make silane which can be used as a fuel. Aluminum and other metals from the moon could be used in numerous ways for building space stations, solar mirrors or any number of other things. Pure silicon could be used in the weightless environment of space to grow perfect crystals from which wafers can be cut on which to etch solar cells or sophisticated electronic circuitry. It's my bet that a guarantee of a steady flow of any sort of material into earth orbit would spur private industry to build not only stations but factories in orbit. Meanwhile back on the moon the same process which make the solar arrays to drive our dinky catapult would continue to operate, making possible larger catapults and other high energy technology feasible.

With the dream of the orbital refueling station mostly satisfied it will be a simpler and less expensive matter to mount a mission to one of Mars's moon or to an asteroid. The upper stage of a craft which has climbed up from earth, when refueled, will be able to complete a trip to Mars and back. Whether there will be significant settlements on Mars within the next century is still an open question. Mars seems to be less and less hospitable the more we look at it and the pervasive ultra-fine particle dust on the moon appears to be highly problematic for persons wishing to pass in and out of a surface habitat. I suspect as many have before me, that a great many of the persons residing in space will live either on asteroids which provide structural material as well as support for solar mirrors, or in rotating habitats. Once built such spacegoing communities could be gradually and in various ways, moved to different orbits, even from planet to planet and could be used for mounting operations on Mars, in asteroid clusters or even the moons of the outer planets.

In order to move about to any great extent in deep space we'll need something more than chemical rockets or thrusters powered by solar cells. Solar arrays get very large quite rapidly when we start talking about propelling significant payloads around at miles per second. Again, our answer is likely the moon. For very high velocity travel in space it's hard to beat ultra-powerful lasers which can push things along literally with light pressure, or matter beams; streams of little bullets shot from ultrafast catapults to swarm toward a receding spaceship and be vaporized just behind the ship, their momentum being soaked up by an electromagnet which allows the ship to be accelerated rather than being incinerated by the energetic plasma generated. Ultimately I believe this will be to way we'll send large payloads around the solar system or achieve velocities of millions of miles per hour.

What about beyond the solar system? Flight to the stars has been debated about as long as spaceflight itself. All methods we know about, short of willing ourselves from world to world or taking advantage of some sort of time-space warp of which we are so far unaware; will be extremely expensive in terms of energy and material. Many science fiction writers have more or less come to the consensus that if starflight occurs it might employ velocities of ten percent the speed of light, about sixty-seven million miles per hour. Since starships with human crews are likely to be big, it's fairly easy to show that using a matter beam to drive a ship of say ten thousand tons, we'll need an array of solar cells on the moon the size of Nevada and the catapult generating the matter beam would likely need to wrap rather around the moon, acting like an enormous cyclotron.

But wait a minute; if we have a power source sufficient to send ten thousand tons of spacecraft to another star an average speed of sixty-seven million miles per hour, we could also send ten starships, each weighing a hundred thousand tons at a bit under seven million miles per hour. Yes, the nearest star would be four hundred years away but we could target ten stars at once. Our catapult would be more modest, requiring a length of perhaps only 6,500 miles, about once around the moon. The matter beams would be easier to generate and would need to travel shorter distances to get their ships up to terminal velocity.

Who would sign on to a space mission lasting from four hundred to perhaps a thousand years? It's possible that by the time we have enormous strays of solar cells on the moon and the ability to generate huge beams of ultra-energized matter, we may look at the universe and our lives in it with different eyes. A significant fraction of the human race may already be residing in self-contained habitats and communication between those spacegoing city stations may well be more significant than that with Old Earth. The first few years or even decades of life aboard a starship being one of several heading to diverging destinations in the galaxy wouldn't need to be much different than life in a solar space city. There'd still be communication back and forth and perhaps even a certain amount of transport from one to the other. Some sort of suspended animation might turn out to be possible, allowing many persons to sleep through much of the journey or there is the possibility of teleportation which would make the speed at which a starship is traveling rather moot because one might visit other ships, even Earth and the other planets at will.

No I'm not suggesting we'll ever be able to send copies of

ourselves atom by atom either as laser light or pure information, to be reconstructed somewhere else. What I am suggesting is that through the use of nanotechnology and other techniques of the not-to-distant future, we may be able to simultaneously assess the immediate states of all the neuronal cells in our bodies and send that information as a dense data stream to a location possibly lightyears away. At that destination the brain/nerve pattern would be set up in an artificial body, constructed or synthesized to accept and conform to the data sent and activate the interactive cellular pattern in its own part biological, part machine cells. The original body of the teleported traveler might well have been destroyed in the scanning and transmitting process and a person would essentially wake up in the constructed destination body.

Would such a person be the original, the one who was originally *sent?* Would the person even be human? A debate to dwarf the abortion issue will rage over the next few centuries. If the process works however and I think eventually someone will try it; it would seem that once scanned it would be easier to move from one construct body to the other because the artificial bodies would be so constructed to be more easily scanned than our tender human bodies will likely be. There's no reason why the artifact bodies shouldn't be more rugged and live a good deal longer than our current meatware and when one is about to die, there seems to be nothing wrong with hopping to a new body. It'll make for a bit of an overpopulation problem so those folks keen on transferring to these artifact bodies really should be required to migrate out-system! Looking at our political analysis, human teleportation turns out to be a Level One issue like genetic engineering and spaceflight itself, in the province of experts which we'd expect it to be. We could curtail research of course but I expect some government or very rich commercial enterprise will try it one day.

Before human teleportation is tried though, we'll have a lot of fun teleporting first robotic organisms in full motion, then simple animals, then those more complex. Were my beloved dog about to die, would I not contemplate seeing if her simulacrum acted the same, was as affectionate and might live to a span to rival mine?

So we have a view of the future in space, a leisurely outmigration to many destinations simultaneously, perhaps transmitting ourselves back and forth and between with the ultimate reward of a network of human colonies in unhurried but constant contact with one another. I like the shape of that. We need more time to mature and we need time to make ourselves the sort of people, the sort of society that we'd want to meet whatever neighbors we might have.

I think we can realize most or all of those goals if we have the desire, but before we build the huge lunar arrays of solar cells and the matterbeam generators we need to learn about the biology and sociology, the ecology and psychology of living in small, rather insular communities distanced from the parent planet and how to prepare for a life in which little or no physical work may be required of most of us. To prepare for that we must seek deeper understanding of our environment on earth, our social structures and our own minds and the best way to bring that about is through the free exchange of ideas, scientific, social, political and personal. We must ask ourselves what it means to be alive, a member of society and sentient. What is this thing called Human and how different are we really from other living things in the Universe and from one another.

--And by the way-- what *about* The Environment? Not all space enthusiasts harbor the dream of leaving earth for some distant home in this or some other solar system. Jeff Bezos, founder of

Blue Origin, a human space flight start-up company, envisions a time when most or all major industries will be moved out into orbit where finished products can be turned out at whatever rate we desire without further harming our fragile ecosystem here on Earth. This planet could potentially become a place of parks and woodlands, unsullied rivers, streams, lakes and oceans. Far from being adversaries then, the ecologist could help the dedicated workforce detailed to manage things beyond the planet, teaching them how to stay alive and healthy in there spacegoing manufactories, while the sustained effort of space technologists will give our planet (as much as is possible) back to Nature.

Chapter 10.

Ultimate Destinies

Before closing this book it's appropriate to ask, what is it we want as individuals and as a race? Asking the question makes obvious the futility of coming to any one answer, but is there some means of arriving at a range of outcomes which could satisfy everyone?

Some of us love wide-open spaces while some cherish the bustle and excitement of large cities. Probably most of us enjoy some of both though in different proportions. Technological trends underway right now, could lead in one direction to monolithic residential structures packing an entire city in a single building. In another direction, telepresence could make it possible for us to interact and work while being scattered across the globe, perhaps in nearly self-contained family habitats. Our industrial capacities could be increased to manufacture ever more enormous structures, vehicles and utilities or it could be shrunk and distributed so each of us could have charge of the things which touch our lives.

It's possible that people who were born around 1950 have seen greater changes to this planet than any other generation in the history of our race. Many of us knew personally individuals who could remember what we call The Old West with its gunfights, cattle drives and wars between natives and settlers.

Where once there were small towns, unincorporated suburbs and open country there are now cities, municipal agglomerations and shopping centers. Whether global warming is responsible or not, our weather has changed. Seattle frequently experiences snow and temperatures well below freezing, while Michigan often receives only sparse snow. The Southern United States is subject to blizzards and frozen roads. The Gulf Coast is becoming a place of annually occurring peril. Our schools have become places of camera surveillance where the threat of mass murder constantly hovers. Even in fairly decent parts of our cities homeless people are regularly seen. At the same time, our phones have come loose from the wall and travel about with us. A child of four can possess in a toy with more computing power than the US Government possessed in 1950. We routinely communicate with individuals all around the world and at any time of day or night. We do extraordinary things with sound, pictures, even solid artifacts.

So what's good and what's bad about what we've done so far, what we can do and what we will soon be able to do? Those of us who still remember clean air and water and food free of salmonella and e. Coli will say that air, water and soil pollution is definitely a negative. The loss of much of our woodlands and open countryside is another. Cell phones and Facebook may be irritating but the ability to keep track of each other and to summon help when needed is probably a positive. Most of us would like to be disease free but how much intervention do we wish the medical industry to have in our private lives? We like being able to get where we're going when we want to but do we want to live along a major traffic corridor such as I-5?

It's likely impossible to please everyone but I suspect we'd all appreciate a cleaner environment, some choice in the continuum between country and city for residence and probably point to point transport without resorting to freeways and airports. Most of us probably like having what we want to eat when we want to eat it. This is why it's kind of hard to find commonalities for all societies and all people.

In large measure we all like what we like because it's what we're used to, so if we raised a generation of humans all having the same sorts of environments and resources would that unify us as humans in our desires and aspirations, and would this be a reasonable or even a moral thing to do? I suspect the answer to the first question is probably no. The range of desires and ambitions we find within any significant sample of human beings tends to indicate that we'll always exhibit differences in how we wish to live, spend our time and expend efforts. As to the other question, well, isn't that what totalitarianism is really all about?

Visions for humanity's future as postulated in science fiction are varied and sometimes surprisingly creative. Robert Silverberg envisioned a world in which cities were single structures hundreds of stories high, dotting and hermetically sealed against a landscape given over to farming and agrarian life. The monad, 113 stories tall, appeared in Galaxy Magazine in the early 1970s. Clifford D. Simak envisioned a world of futuristic RV parks where landing spaces accommodated solar-powered dwellings, moving about the world by means of antigravity. Kenneth Bulmer in his book Worlds For the Taking wrote of city ships, interstellar craft with hundreds of thousands or millions of people aboard, traveling through the galaxy more or less indefinitely. It seems though that most science fiction visions tend toward either the super city or the distributed agrarianism. To me the two most attractive prospects for the far future would be a wooded planet with lots of interesting animals, lakes, rivers, mountains and oceans and the large space city in orbit, the two linked by reusable rockets, probably fueled with solar-generated hydrogen and oxygen; or a multitude of planetary settlements, ranging from backwoods to urban, linked across the lightyears by some sort of teleport network. Presently I enjoy living on three acres which are only a few miles from a reasonably-sized community. That's my viewpoint and I realize it's probably not yours.

Something I think we need to at least try to agree on before each of us building our individual visions of the future, is the matter of computers. It has become an article of faith (largely through constant repetition I think, in the manner of The Big Lie (a well known technique of propaganda) that computers have radically altered our culture by making various social and business functions easier and more efficient. Though I realize I'll likely be pilloried, I politely reply *bunk!* It's my feeling that computers, though sometimes allowing us to do things more precisely, have mostly allowed us to do merely *more* of the various things we'd always done before. Computerization makes it easy to document more verbosely what we do in business, politics or social services, but is the increase in documentation really a good thing? Computerization in connection with the internet allows us to respond directly to messages and also respond to some potentially huge group of other persons (interested or not) but is that really necessary? Computerization allows us to approximate any mathematical process but does it help us understand the underlying mathematics?

I don't mean to say that we shouldn't have computers and that they don't do good things. It would be highly risky to calculate interplanetary trajectories, design nuclear reactors or do gene mapping without computers. Experts appear to need computers and agencies charged with public safety such as meteorological bureaus, geophysical surveys and the federal communications commission need computers.

Beyond this, what do computers really do for us? Most of the computer power used by private individuals has to do with communication and writing, as well as playing various sorts of games. I don't have a big problem with any of these functions. What I do have a problem with is the constant pressure by computer manufacturers to push the technology ever faster and ever more complex so every couple of years we're expected to buy new computers with new software. The more complex our computers become, the more subject we are to computer viruses. These rogue programs, evidently written by persons obsessed with ego-self-stimulation, cause so much trouble for business or governmental functions that it is a valid question how much time do computers truly save?

For most of us, it's nice to be able to send E-mail messages or word-process a document. It's also nice to go on the internet and look up the molecular mass of silicon-dioxide or the first occurrence of a steam-powered vehicle but how much of a computer do we really need to do that? It appears to me that a web-service such as Wikipedia is a good example. A fledgling beginning of Isaac Asimov's Encyclopedia Galactica, Wikipedia makes a vast amount of cross-referenced information available to a fairly modest computer. It doesn't take a lot of computer power to send an e-mail or to word-process a story, essay or even an entire book. I'm saying that we should freeze the internet and a majority of computers sold for public consumption. Let's sell computers that will be valid and usable for at least a decade. This viewpoint won't be popular, hence my pillorying; but computer manufacturers have held us to ransom long enough!

There is a scientific and well as a practical and ideological reason to take a hard look at computerization. When we travel to the stars, we'll need not only to make the things we need to survive but to make the tools we need to make the things we need to survive. Though I believe we could build a fabber--3-D printer--

which functions by taking apart a master copy and turning out two replicas of the master; I'm not sure that fabbers will successfully be able to reproduce computer chips. What if we travel to the stars but can't take our computers with us? I'm not sure it would be a bad thing!

Chapter 11.

Dreaming the Old One's Dream

The air here in the morning smells like Earl gray tea. By afternoon it takes on a roasted character. Think of caramel corn. At night it's a cool spearmint. There are waves of grassland here which my anaerobic digester gulps down along with my own contributions, to furnish me with biogas and fertilizer for my integrated greenhouse. The grass yields seeds with thin husks which grinds into a nutty bread flour.

Most of the people here headed right away for the choice spots, along the coast or by some of the lakes. I'm about 30 K up this river from the so, where neighbors are spare and something to be savored when chance met rather than kept at distance.

I've got a little boat, a rowing craft; 'just messing about in boats' as The Rat said. I could easily enough swim the river in my amplifier with the visor down but what's the hurry. Cliff Simak lives down the river about a Klick and we go fishing now and again, just gentle friends on the water. Cliff's Towser likes playing with my Sally Dog. She's a Blue Heeler with the white Bentley mark on her forehead. She somehow showed up here when I did though I don't know why. She wasn't with me when it happened.

Lazarus Long lives further down the valley with his clan of adopted many-time Great grand descendants. I've been out hunting with him a few times and we enjoy swapping stories but I dislike killing. I don't use firearms any longer because making gunpowder is tedious and it doesn't grow local. I've got a pneumatic crossbow which can throw a lead slug like a rifle and relies ultimately on my own strength. There's a below-the-barrel spring-loaded dart for emergencies.

Back up the rise near where the woodland starts, Zenna Henderson lives and constitutes a sort of one-woman welcoming service for aliens, which of course we all must be. She's good company and always good for a chat and a cup of tea. About twenty minutes fast walk from Zenna, Andre Norton keeps a little chalet and seems to be doing some sort of psychic research. There are others, many others but my neighboring needs are minimal yet sharp enough to cherish a friend.

When we finally went back to The Moon, Earth's Moon in 2027 everyone onsite was involved with the construction of the Base. It took some telepresence explorers and it was a year or more before The Portal was discovered. Information discovered onsite and decoded through the brute might of quantum computing indicated that the builders or founders or conjurers of The Portal Gate were our ancestors, or at least a parent race who'd brought our seed from Elsewhere. I can't claim to understand the workings of the Gateway though I understand about its carrying capacity and the sporadic nature of it's connecting with places elsewhere which makes communication with the old home a happenstance thing, but that's all right.

When it came my turn I was shown into a huge warehouse, or that's the closest I can come to describing. I wasn't actually shown, more like just put there. I had a sense that anything known to our benefactor race was here and all I need do was to think about categories to fill the room with anything fitting that notion or nearly so. I knew I could have whatever I wanted, but only that which could pass through the portal. (I built the boat myself, something I'd always wanted to do.)

I never really meant to apply to go off-planet. it's just that I'd spent my life dreaming, calculated and writing about space so when real space transport opened up and the bottom more or less fell out of not only NASA but the various commercial space ventures, tickets to orbit were dirt cheap (Well orbital habitat dirt cheap). I threw half my savings into a private ticket to LEO figuring I'd like to feel what John Glenn and Ed White and Neil Armstrong had known in the early rocket days. I guess I didn't make it. One second I was feeling the crushing press of Q-max thrusting, the jets screaming in my earphoned ears. The next, I was someplace else. Then there was that great hall or warehouse or maybe it's what super races have instead of shopping malls.

I've got my greenhouse/workshop Habitat with a little sleeping room down at the end for me and facilities that communicate with the digester. I can grow all the salad and table vegetables I need and Sally seems adept at catching what she wants from the field or even in low-flying airspace. She also loves hot bread and the occasional dish of bean chili.

My amplifier suit allows me to travel ten times as fast as I can walk yet allows me to exert my muscles to whatever degree I wish and it's sun (star?) charged.

There's also a fabricator which somehow takes rocks apart and can copy anything I give it, making two copies so the broken original can be replaced. Neighbors borrow things from one another a fair amount, not flour or salt or a chunk of fire but whole bottles and intact tools. Still things don't break all that much. Oh yes, speaking of bottles, I found I could malt and brew the prairie grass seed to make a not half-bad Porter. I guess I don't need excellent.

There seem to be nano-repair bots which keep the amplifier suit in repair and possibly me as well because I've experienced no physical distress since I've arrived here, though admittedly, it's not been all that long. Of course the fabber can make copies of itself or more importantly, someone else's fabber can accomplish the same.

What do I do with myself besides fishing and the occasional hunt and brisk walkabouts? My other lifetime fascination was the workings, if you will, the physics of social systems and historical processes. I was in high school when I first drew up a chart of what I considered to be major historical turning points and started extracted predictive data to try and foresee how things might fall out in the next fifty years or so. Of course with only one world to study one could never be sure if any pattern posited had any intrinsic validity or was merely some assumed pattern imposed upon randomness. Here I have the histories of many worlds, many solar systems to study and compare. Think of an encyclopedia in which every page, every word, every character opens out into a new and different Britannica.

There's this head-mounted thing, I call it my curiosity cap. Just a couple of contacts which rest against the temples and a band to keep them in place. It doesn't truly help one to think in the conventional sense but to amplify curiosity. Long ago I defined a living system as one that was "curious." I went on to define curiosity as spontaneous pattern-seeking. Put a robot with a general operating program on a river bed and if it starts without direct command to go up and down river, observing the current, looking at rocks, making comparisons apprehending anomalies and seeking their sources then it is curious and by implication, conscious. The test is to move the robot to the desert then the prairie and see if it behaves the same, in a manner appropriate to locale.

I guess it's something like that with my curiosity cap and perhaps it has a consciousness of its own. I'm not sure. It's hard to explain but when I'm looking at a very great deal of data it seems to help me find patterns as if I suddenly see a trail through the forest which I can follow. I have to do the following and I can take turns, retrace and try again but I can access much more information at a time than I could ever hold in my head before and it's useful in solving complex differential equations too!

No one else in my family appears to be here, at least not yet except for Sally of course and she's a little blue anomaly as she was presumably laying around on the couch while I was off rocketing away to my demise (and my transcendence). There are some here who have wives, husbands, parents, children but some who might have but don't. The general consensus when we speak of it is that   some of our loved ones may have just taken another path.   We seemed to be matched to our destination by temperament. We may well meet again someday if not in this form, then in some other. That's fine.

I guess it's an open secret that we can start things over for ourselves, each of us, pretty much any time we please. I've thought about that a fair amount. Things have changed so much, back home and elsewhere and there are so many, many planets. In order to truly understand an entirely new state of affairs one really needs to be born into it, growing up soaking in the social implications. That's an interesting thought. We spend so damned much time though relearning what perhaps we once knew, I wonder if there really is anything to the reincarnation idea? I would cheerfully return again to the womb and the cradle with all that implies if at some appropriate time, I could bequeath to myself all that I know now. A psionicist chap who happened to be sojourning at Andre's house when I happened by one day said it may well be possible to do something like that and he's apparently working on it. I guess we'll have to wait and see.

For the now, I'm healthy, content enough and seem to have the time to learn whatever I wish if I want it badly enough, if I'm truly "curious."

I gaze out the transparent panel of my greenhouse garden at the triple staffs standing near the river's, down by my little dock. There are flags of The United States the old 50-star; a flag of the Confederacy with its crossing red stripes (misnomer really, the correct term is Battle Flag) and the Lion, Crown and Unicorn of Scotland. I touch my forehead where the peak of a cap might be, and Remember.

Appendix A.

Inverting the Issues:

In Chapter 2. we looked at a list of socio-political issues, evaluating them in terms of four principles of moral behavior or social good/ harm. We showed that they tended to fall into one of four categories, ie. 0. Nothing you can do about it, 1. Province of expert or Government, 2. Special interest and 3. Subject to personal decision or popular vote. The issues examined are shown with their ratings as follows.

Abortion	0
Gun control	0
War	0
Gay Marriage	0
Genetic Engineering	1
Space development	1
Illegal Immigration	2
New oil drilling	2
Social Welfare	3
Environmental Protection	3
Evolution Education	3
Hybrid Cars	3

Renewable Energy	3
Taxation	3
Transgender Rights	3

We also said that we could take an inverse of an issue making a positive into a negative or restriction and vice versa as follows:

Ban Abortions

1. Does it hurt anybody? Yes. Some women lose their lives without such medical intervention. 2. Would it be bad if everyone was denied an abortion? Yes, for same reason as 1. 3. If abortion was generally illegal would it be a social evil if no one was ever allowed one? Yes. 0. Can we do anything about it? Not really. Rating One converted to Zero.

Assure gun rights for all

1. Would this hurt anyone? Yes. Some persons are not competent to own and handle guns. Small children, persons with severe mental illness, persons with dementia, incompetent persons. 2. Would it be a bad thing if everyone owned a gun? That's likely because of 1. 3. If most people owned guns would it be a bad thing if some did not? An argument might be made but generally I'd say no. 0. Can we do anything about it? No. Rating Two converted to Zero.

Decrease military spending

1. Does it do harm? Yes. It can, depending on the degree of reduction and the current world situation. 2. If military spending was generally curtailed by everyone would this be harmful. Probably because there are always threats in the land. 3. If

spending was generally curtailed for military activities would it be a bad thing if some people supported the military or participated with it. No because it appears that some military activities and therefore support is essential. 0. Can we do anything about it? We probably cannot prevent war but we can cut spending. Rating Two.

Ban gay Marriage

1. Does it hurt anyone? Yes, the gay people in question would feel harmed. 2. If all gay marriages were banned would this be a social evil? I believe gay people who wished to be married would feel harmed. 3. If all gay marriages were banned would it be bad if some gay people got married anyway? No, probably not. if gay marriages were generally banned but a few mavericks married anyway it wouldn't change much of anything even though society had determined such unions to be wrong. 0. Can we do anything about it? Sure. Rating 2. (We see this takes us from the one or expert category on the positive rating scale to the Two or special interest category on the Negative Scale.)

Ban Genetic Engineering

1. Does it hurt anyone? I believe so because there is a lot of benefit to be gained from the field even though there is a potential downside. 2. If everyone banned or refrained from genetic engineering would that be a social evil? I believe so, for the same reason. 3. If Genetic engineering was generally banned would it but negative if some persons didn't break the law and practice it anyway? I believe so because even if for no other reason than to know how to apply sensible controls some investigation into genetic engineering is essential. Zero. Can we do anything about it? Yes. Rating Three.

Ban oil drilling

1. A total ban on oil drilling could be harmful because petroleum is needed for many important purposes. 2. If everyone foreswore oil drilling we'd have the same as 1, so Yes. 3. If everyone generally avoided drilling for oil, would it be a social evil if no one drilled for oil? Yes. As with genetic engineering, there would need to be some exceptions. 0. Can we do anything? Yes. Rating Three.

Ban space development

1. Would this hurt anyone? Yes. Without weather and navigation satellites, many lives would be lost. Also a total ban would lose jobs for a lot of highly-trained workers. 2. If everyone participated in a general ban of space development it would be negative because of 1. 3. If there existed a general ban on space development would it be a social evil if there wasn't someone working on the problems of space travel and development? Not really, because the situation won't be affected by lone mavericks. 0. Can we do anything about it? Yes. Rating Two. (We observe a shift by inverting the issue from a category One issue to a Special interest matter.)

Enforce Immigration laws

1. Certainly some people would be hurt, particularly refugees and those unable to earn a living at home. 2. If everyone strictly enforced immigration laws then government prescribed regulations covering immigration to this country would be evenly enforced. 3. Skip. 0. yes. Rating One. (We've gone from Special Interest to Expert through inverting this issue.)

Cut welfare benefits

1. This would be harmful to many people who depend on government subsidies and may have no apparent alternate for support. 2. If every State and county cut welfare spending, it could be harmful because of question 1. 3. If welfare benefits were cut, would it be a social evil if no one worked to provide recipients with cash and resources? Yes, it's called charitable giving. 0. yes. Score Three.

Rescind Environmental protection regulations

1. This appears to be going on in America at this point in time and I believe it is harmful. 2. If everyone abandoned environmental protection rules or regulations this would be a social evil. 3. If everyone generally ignored environmental protection protocols would it be a social evil if some persons practiced protection anyway? No, because a few voices crying in the wilderness can't accomplish much if after all of this time the entire country is determined to rescind. 0. Yes. Our Type One issue is now flipped to a Special Interest item. Rating Two.

Ban the teaching of evolution in school

1. Would deprive students of some informative and powerful information and theoretical science, whether or not it covers all facts or answers all questions satisfactorily. 2. If the teaching of Evolution was generally banned, a social evil would occur because of 1. 3. If Evolution education is generally banned would it be a social evil if no one spoke about it or taught the material? Yes. To suppress this would constitute mind control. 0. Can we do anything? Probably. Score Three.

Ban sale of hybrid automobiles

1. This would certainly be bad for the manufacturers of hybrids and most certainly for the environment. 2. If everyone chose to boycott or were prevented from buying hybrids, a social evil would occur because of 1. 3. If hybrid cars were generally banned would it be wrong if a few people didn't build and drive them anyway? Not really because a few hybrid cars can't affect the overall national or global situation. 0. Yes. Rating Two.

Cut funding for renewable energy development

1. Yes, we desperately need cleaner renewable sources of energy and conservation does not appear to be adequate to the energy-shortage situation. 2. If everyone participated in a renewable energy ban, yes for the same reason. 3. If almost nobody used renewable energy would it be an evil if a few hold-outs didn't continue its use? Not particularly, because a few people won't make a big difference and if the government has a good and sufficient reason to support oil, then any object value energy dissidents might have would only contribute to civil disobedience. 0. Yes. Rating Two.

Cut taxes

1. This could be harmful if sufficient revenue is not available to fund necessary government programs. 2. If everyone's taxes were cut would this be a social evil? Not necessarily. Society might adjust to take care of more formerly governmental functions in alternate ways. 3. Skip. 0. Yes. Rating One.

Ban affirmative action for transgendered persons

1. People in this category would be harmed. 2. If everyone ignored Trans Rights harm would occur to not only the folks in question but I think, make us a culturally poorer society. 3. If most people ignored Trans Rights would it be a social evil if some people were not supportive? Yes. In a case like this, a few can make a big difference. 0. Yes. Rating Three.

It's difficult to extract general rules to cover all permutations seen when going from the initial issue to the inversion but there tends to be a drift toward special interests when we impose a negative, restricting, curtailing, banning rather than suggesting, expanding, providing.

Appendix B.

Calculation of solar array size for pocket Biosphere in Chapter 4.

We start with a daily caloric food value to feed an adult person of 2,000 nutritional calories which is actually two million heat energy calories in the Metric system, equaling 8.36 million joules. If plants use light energy at about one percent efficiency, we multiply our value by one hundred to represent the daily amount of light energy required to allow plants to generate the amount of food needed per person. This is 836 million joules. We won't be able to eat all of what we grow so we'll assume an optimistic sixty percent edible mass per average plant so our energy bill is now 1.4 billion joules per day.

We'll assume the grow lights we are using will convert electricity to light at about thirty percent efficiency so we divide 1,400,000,000 by 0.30 and obtain 4,666,666,666 or about 4.67 billion joules. Since we are assuming that sunshine will be available 300 days per year, we take the ratio 300/365.25 and get about .82 which we divide into the above figure and get 5.69 billion joules of electricity needed per average day to feed one person. Multiplying this by eight for the number of occupants we are envisioning we now have 45.53 billion joules or 12,650 KWH per day. If we are using this energy eight hours per day, approximately the time sun will be available in a Southern Latitude, we must generate electricity at the rate of 1,581 kilowatts.

Solar cells generating at about ten percent efficiency, sunlight to electric power; requiring about ten square meters of surface to generate a kilowatt or 15,810 to generate 1,581 KW. 15,810 square meters *knowledge* 170'160.50 square feet and as one acre is 43,560 square feet, we divide by 43,560 to get 3.91 acres. This is a circular area about four hundred and sixty-five feet across, a bit larger than the entire Biosphere II Installation, but covered mostly with photo voltaic cells.

Appendix C.

Another look at The Unborn

The very fact that I would presume to discuss the rights of the unborn or responsibilities of mothers in any context will be offensive to many but because the controversy over abortion is such a hotly contested one, people tend to talk past one another and listening is seldom to be found. I don't expect anyone to give credence to my opinions either. I hope not so much to set forth opinions here, but to catalog the universe of possible opinions so to gain some perspective and any conclusion reached may be reached by each person, not merely postulated by me.

When I was in high school I read doctor David Reuben's somewhat jocular, often disturbing book Everything You Always Wanted To Know About Sex But Were Afraid To Ask. It contained a chapter on abortion which I found to be horrific, not so much that abortions were performed, but what happened to women who could not obtain safe, medically competent abortions. At that point I decided that if anything, I was pro-choice at least up to a point (I was a six-month baby myself and my cousin a five-month.)

At the beginning of my Junior year in college I had a rather acrimonious debate one evening with my roommate who was decrying feminism because "they believe in abortion and that is obviously wrong." Terry said that the baby had a soul which began at the time of conception because there was no other obvious point at which to locate the event. Killing any fetus at any age, he declared, was murder. Like most strictures decreed by celibate men with no practical experience in dealing with fetuses, this has the elegance of simplicity and seeming logical impeccability.

Of course any OB-GYN nurse will tell you that women

spontaneously abort fertilized eggs "embryos" all the time so if the soul is such a crucial matter for an ever-vigilant deity, this would seem a strange arrangement of affairs. Of course the spontaneous abortion argument doesn't entirely refute the existence of soul at conception, because in elective abortion there is the element of intentionality. Spontaneous abortions can be chalked up to God's Will.

Before I go on though, I want to say something about the soul itself and in general. I didn't really think much about its existence apart from the conscious mind until I was about twenty-one. Indeed all I'd learned up till this time tended toward a body/mind duality with spirit or probably soul synonymous with mind or consciousness. Around the time I was having my row with Terry my roommate, I was taking a new and harder look at religion and exploring matters which I'd previous more or less dismissed as nonsense. One of these matters was the soul as something defining a person as a conscious, feeling, uniquely-experiencing being, apart from the mere information stored within the brain. I like the analogy of a flame being passed from candle to candle. It's a different candle now but the same flame.

Previously I guess I'd sort of thought that in some higher-dimensional fashion my thoughts and personality might be transmitted at time of death to the mind of god or perhaps to another body or home of the mind. If the soul is like a flame and has touched my mind/body continuum at some point, probably in the womb, did it not exist before I was born? If it is reputed to survive after my body and brain have ceased to function would this not bespeak an indestructibility or conservation of the soul? It might change, grow, presumably even shrink, but like energy, it could not be entirely destroyed.

I said to my roommate during our lengthy argument that if one assumed that every embryo was regarded to possess a soul then this would forbid a person taking a clone of self and moving mind into it. He was horrified and wondered why anyone would even think of such a thing. Obviously I'm not the only one who has.

An interesting point arises here. The term "Unborn" can mean human cloning and mind transfer as well as a growing fetus. When we think about it, the arguments which apply to one apply just as well to the other. I believe current doctrine in speculative science circles mandates that a clone intended for a "body transplant" must be kept in either a sensory-deprived state until time to make the mind transfer or be in constant contact with the clone donor via a neuro-electronic link of some kind so the two would continue to be uniquely identical. This may answer some of the questions relating to identical twins and the strange and amazing sorts of rapport they tend to have. They may in their similarity be so close to the one person that they function in many ways as one person even though great distances may separate them. An analogy can be found in the phenomenon of Quantum Entanglement of electrons which is beyond the scope of this book but means that once electrons have been associated with one another in some way, one electron moved far away from the other, will display the effects of whatever is done to the other electron. (It's spooky stuff.)

It turns out that over the millennia there've been a variety of views on when life actually begins. In the middle ages some authorities spoke of the time of quickening when the mother first felt she was experiencing a life within her. Other authorities in other cultures said that a child without a name couldn't be considered to truly have a soul. Some African tribes I'm told, claimed that a child had no soul until after the first anniversary of its birth. Some races or sexes were held by certain philosophers as having no soul at all.

Dr. Carl Sagan proposed that as an attempt at compromise between the warring factions on the abortion front we that set the time of life's beginning and therefore the soul if any, at the time the middle brain develops as that seems to be the seat of consciousness and emotion. This apparently occurs at about seven weeks.

Of course missing one period happens from time to time for many women. Missing two is probably significant but the seven-week "safe time" has already been exceeded. I think if elective abortions are to be legal they need to at least but available through the first trimester of gestation. I don't feel real comfortable about that but to offer anything less would be to make war on my sisters and I cannot do that.

I've heard some women say that they had a right to abort a fetus up until the time that it could survive outside of their bodies and that time is identified differently depending on the person making the declaration. I'm not moved by arguments like that. If I can swim and you can't and we fall off a ship am I justified in swimming away, leaving you behind? Perhaps if I know that I can't possibly assist you in any meaningful way but if I feel able to help you, I should. If a woman at any time during her pregnancy is endangered by the bearing of a fetus then she should have the option of terminating the pregnancy by abortion if necessary or surgical removal of the baby if possible. As we become better able to take unbirthed infants from the womb and nurture them to proper birth condition, possibly in an artificial womb, I think we should do that. I think that a reasonable and compassionate society should allow abortions probably with some attempt at counseling, during trimester O. I'm opposed to any third trimester abortions and am willing to fight for the rights of those children, for they are children, not just blobs of matter. I feel abortions in the second trimester should only be done for compelling medical reasons. This gives everyone a chance to be angry at me.

When I returned to church at about age 27, our pastor gave a talk on abortion with the assistance of a young female theologian who had studied this issue in connection with the Christian Church. Pastor Weir summed up by saying "It is my personal belief that in every case abortions are wrong. It is also my belief that in all cases we must treat persons who elect to have abortions with love and understanding. We are not called to harm those with whom we disagree."

I guess I stand a bit more in the Pro-choice direction than Norm Weir but I respect what he said as I've also respected a good deal of what others have said, including my roommate Terry. As I've said elsewhere, when society tells a woman to bear a child who is not financially able to do so, then society assumes responsibility for that pregnancy and that mother, at least for a time. We're quick to tell people what to do but not always so eager to support those people when they run into difficulty following our mandates.

The last argument I made to Terry was that if the soul is indestructible then if someone decides to have an abortion, possibly not understanding the significance of soul and the beginning of life, God could take up that soul and put it somewhere else. He told me that he'd never heard anything as goofy as that. Well a lot of people believe in transmigration of souls. Even the judeo-Christian/Islamic view of afterlife constitutes a transmigration of sorts, does it not?

The only real mention of life before birth that I've found in The Bible is in the Gospel according to Luke Chapter 1. Mary is with child and travels to visit her cousin Elizabeth. Elizabeth is pregnant with whom will become John the Baptist. John jumps in his mother's womb when Mary draws near. Could be coincidence. It's generally assumed that Elizabeth could have been not much more than six months pregnant at this time though it could have been earlier. We don't know. Abortion is a topic concerning which we can't afford to be cavalier any more than any other issue affecting human life, but if the soul is indestructible it must live on somewhere, somehow and if not, our definition of soul as espoused by the major world religions looks to be invalid. Let us please endeavor to be kind to one another and to seek understanding to the extent we are able.

Appendix D.

The Potential of Small Scale Biomass

Growing green plants as a source of fuel has been a hotly debated issue on the energy scene for half a century or more. Of course for much of history Humanity depended on fuel sources such as wood, peat dried dung and the like but we weren't industrialized then so cooking and winter warming were the major thermal energy needs of the average home. The steam engine changed all that. Some people have speculated that had the Roman Empire needed to deal with nearly total deforestation and had turned to coal, a practical steam engine might have been developed 1,800 years earlier than it actually was. I'm not proposing biomass energy as a replacement for the major energy sources currently running our industry but examining it as an at-home energy source, integrated not only into household infrastructure but in the environment as well.

There was a lot of excitement during the 1970s about making alcohol from surplus grains, sugar beets and seed-producing plants such as sunflowers. About thirty years later gasahol, a mixture of gasoline with ten percent ethyl alcohol became standard for much of the nation's automotive fuel supply.

It's probably unfortunate for biomass research generally that emphasis was so much on automotive fuel. Ethanol production is one of the most expensive ways to get energy out of biomass though there are some advantages. The fermentation process yields an high protein mash useful for animal feed and often edible even for humans. The fermentation process also gives off carbon dioxide which can be used for carbonating water or blowing through greenhouses to increase crop yield. A lot of heat is required to first convert starch in grain or potatoes into sugars then the "mash" must be cooled for fermentation which generates heat of its own though at low temperature. Following fermentation a good deal more heat needs to be added to distill the alcohol. All this heat can be reused if one is running a sufficient number of small batches at staggered intervals so one cooling process can act as the heating process for another and a still running more or less continuously would make a good central heating plant for a moderately-sized home or barn but making alcohol also takes a lot of time and requires a lot of labor. Alcohol made at home is best done near a greenhouse and used to run a generator which charges batteries for a car or the house itself, the waste heat from the generator being used for space or water heating. The spent mash from the fermentation process can be fed to chickens, rabbits, goats, cows, hoses etc. which produce manure for greenhouse or garden.

Methyl alcohol can be generated from biomass which needn't be sugary or starchy. It's accomplished by a sort of slow-burning process with steam added which reformulates the cellulose in plants to an alcohol and some byproducts such as water and carbon dioxide as well as organic matter much like compost. Biodiesel can be generated by adding methyl alcohol and sodium or potassium hydroxide to just about any organic master and heating it. This process can yield either a fertilizer or a weed-killer as byproduct depending on whether you use potassium or sodium in the process. Potassium is the fertilizing agent helping seeds and other fruits to form.

A fairly low-temperature process called anaerobic digestion produces carbon dioxide, and methane as well as a number of trace gasses and a fertilizer slurry which can be added the garden, greenhouse beds or algae pond. Digesters tend to be fairly maintenance-intensive and require a lot of preprocessing of material, mixing of manure with water, chopping grass and so forth.

Carbon monoxide can be generated through partial combustion of cellulose with some steam being also formed in the reaction, which can be condensed out. Carbon dioxide can be burned directly for heating or electrical generation or with suitable catalysts and under a certain amount of pressure, can react with water vapor to yield carbon dioxide and free hydrogen. The ideal efficiency of hydrogen production in this method, comparing the energy contained in the biomass with that in the hydrogen generated is about forty-two percent. The remainder of the energy generated is given off as heat. Hydrogen can be used at fairly high efficiencies in electro-chemical fuel cells and is a clean fuel which doesn't degrade fuel cell components as much as some other gaseous or liquid fuels. Generating hydrogen requires a lot of plumbing and control and probably isn't something you'd want to leave running while you were at work or the beach.

Though it's perhaps a bit inelegant, the simplest, most direct and in the long run most efficient way to use biomass from green plants is to just burn it. All plant matter can be pelletized, (ground up, dried and forced through holes in a steel plate to generate little cylinders which look like rabbit food.) These pellets can be feed mechanically at a controlled rate into a small, well-insulated firebox to generate hot combustion gasses which are then fan-forced through a long, narrow channel to heat air flowing in a counterwise channel transferring heat. Since the combustion gasses are traveling in the opposite direction to the air, the gasses exit the heat exchanger at a temperature near that of ambient air and the heated air emerges into the house with about ninety-five percent of the original energy contained in the fuel. If instead of air flowing next to the combustion gasses we had water or another liquid, we'd end up with energetic steam coming out of the heat exchanger and we could run an engine.

There has been a lot of discussion and experimentation over the last few decades relating to Stirling engines which operate by passing air or another gas such as helium back and forth between a heater and a cooler by way of a heat storage device. Efforts with small, home-built Stirlings seem to be hampered by the complexities involved in getting the working fluid to go through the various parts of the engine the back to the starting point to begin a new cycle.   Stirling engines also tend to be fairly large or they must operate at high pressures in order to generate significant amounts of power. A Rankine-type engine in which a liquid is turned to vapor then re-condensed back to liquid (a steam engine) using water or possibly another liquid such as liquid propane or an alcohol will likely generate more power per a given size of engine and possibly at a lower temperature than a comparably-sized Stirling. Such an engine could be designed to keep an hot water tank up to temperature with its waste heat and using auger-fed pellets, could operate pretty much independently. I suspect this sort of system is the best means of utilizing localized biomass energy.   The Rankine engine or for that matter the Stirling, could be designed also to use concentrated solar energy to go on generating through the warm months without expending fuel.

So from where is the biomass coming? The real controversy over biomass energy hasn't really been the manner in which plant matter is to be processed but where and how to grow it. Obviously any vegetation grown for non-nutritional purposes conflicts potentially with crops that are edible. Biomass which is stripped from the land and carried off somewhere to be processed, impoverishes the land because minerals and mulching materials are depleted. Since processing corn or wheat is a lot different than processing sugar beets or potatoes, the tendency is to want to grow large monocultures which can have agriculturally disastrous consequences. What we really need is not one but several crops which can be grown together but are processed in largely the same way, something that can be easily harvested, processed and used onsite, something that allows for the fixation of nitrogen in the soil and something that is mostly cellulose.

There are two obvious examples on land and perhaps two or more in the ocean. Trees can grow about two thirds of a dry ton of new wood per acre per year. Three or so acres of woodlot can keep a family warm through the winter. It's possible to build counterflowing woodstoves which use chunks of split log instead of pellets so in some areas of the country such and Maine, Northern Idaho, anywhere there are still forests, judicious and scientific wood-burning is a reasonable way to go.

Grasses can grow where most other things don't. They form an interactive community comprising many species, many of which fix nitrogen and they are comparatively easy to harvest and process into pellets. Some grasses and brushy plants are quite drought resistant. Per acre yields are all over the map. If you mow your own lawn and want to do something useful for practical biomass technology, keep track of how many hoppers or trash bags full of grass you harvest in a summer (before putting it in your compost pile). Take a representative bag and weigh it. Now take a plastic grocery bag and fill that with newly mowed grass. Get somebody to weigh that. Sometimes the post office will do it for you, possibly a butcher or deli clerk. Take the weighed damp grass, carefully spread it on a cookie sheet and dry it in your oven at no more than 150 degrees F. Put a folded potholder in the crack of the door to let moisture escape. Take the now dried grass and have it reweighed, calculate the percentage of moisture you originally had in your sample, use that percentage to calculate the dry weight of the representative bag. Multiply by the number of bags to get your total dry weight per season and looking at your land deed or Land Entity's, figure out your annual per acre yield. Someone should set up a website for folks who'd like to report and compare.

Neither firewood nor fuel pellets yield nutritional components for animals as does the alcohol process or fertilizer for plants as anaerobic fermentation and biodiesel do. Both firewood and fuel pellets however do leave behind ash which contains the basic minerals from the combusted material and those necessary for the growth of the next generation of trees or grass. Wood ash or grass ash should always be returned where possible, to the original site of harvest, mixed with water so the chemicals soak into the ground. The mulching value of dead plant matter left upon the soil will be diminished by any bioenergy activity but this can be offset to a goodly degree by the use of composting toilets, especially in rural areas. They use no water and render a humus-like end product which can be shoveled once or twice a year into shallow trenches in the lawn, field or tree-lot.

The ocean may well furnish us with a good deal of biofuel energy in the future. One source would be plankton, some species of which are nutritional even for us frail humans. Some species are not so delicious and might be worth harvesting to generate methane and the effluent to be returned to the sea. Another source is giant kelp which may be pelletizable if residual salt isn't too big a problem in combustion. Otherwise they may be useful for making biodiesel. With many species of fish dying back, our coastal waters are likely to become choked with algaes large and small, and using some of it is actually good management of the marine environment. Inland there are milfoils and other fresh water aquatic plants which cost municipalities a good deal each year to keep under control.

Whatever the source, biofuels promise to be a significant player in the local energy game throughout this century and exciting things may be happening in the Pacific Northwest, the Coast of Maine, the Southern pineywoods and the plains of Texas and New Mexico. The greening of America will mean something other than the conflict between tradition, the contemporarily-entrenched and the visionaries of tomorrow. It will mean the most complete and comprehensive use of solar energy and the stewardship of each household's environment.

Let us please walk together toward this future!

The End.

Made in the USA
Columbia, SC
01 February 2021